SMALL CIRCLE JUJITSU

HISTORY & PRACTICE

Oshiego

D0916751

SMALL CIRCLE JUJITSU: HISTORY & PRACTICE

Copyright © 2020 Leon Jay
Stirling Bridge Publications
—Second Edition—
ISBN-10: 0998065420
ISBN-13: 978-0998065427

The material in this book is intended for educational purposes only. No one should undertake the practice of self-defense or healing without qualified instruction and supervision, and an awareness of the criminal and civil limitations on the use of force in self-defense and the practice of medicine. Physical combat is an inherently dangerous activity. Medical diagnosis and treatment should be provided by qualified healthcare professionals. The author, publisher and distributors are not responsible in any manner for any injury or liability that may result from practicing—or attempting to practice—the techniques described herein. Any application of the information contained herein is at the reader's sole and exclusive risk. As a result of the risk of injury to oneself and others, prior to engaging in any type of self-defense program it is advisable to consult both a professional martial arts instructor and a licensed physician.

This book was printed in the United States of America by Stirling Bridge Publications; a publisher specializing in works dedicated to exploring the power of one.

STIRLING
BRIDGE PUBLICATIONS
stirlingbridge@mail.com

Dedicated to the memory of

Professor Wally Jay

Founder of the art of
Small Circle Jujitsu

CONTENTS

FOREWORD
by John Mellon

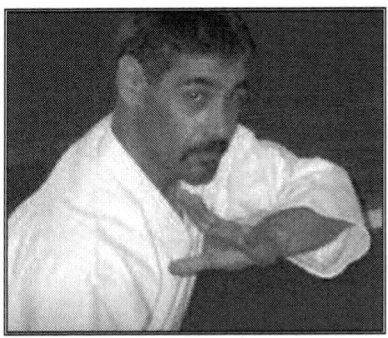

I count it a very fortunate day when I first met Professor Wally Jay at the Second World Jujitsu Championships. A friend of mine—since passed away—was the principal organizer, but almost everything that could go wrong, did. It wasn't his fault; he had an agreement with the London Docklands Development Corporation, a quango created to oversee the development of what later became a whole new financial and corporate center with many leisure facilities, out of the old commercial and industrial docks around the Thames River. They had promised that a state-of-the-art sports complex would be built on the site by the time of the Championships; instead, we arrived on the opening day to be greeted by what was essentially an old industrial hangar, a foot deep in dust and debris. Over the previous few days we had begged and borrowed bleacher seating and mats—I was amazed at the forbearance and graciousness of all the visiting international masters, in particular, Professor Wally.

I had been studying the Professor's book: <u>Dynamic Jujitsu</u>, and I approached him rather shyly at the end of the first day's competition with a question about one of the techniques described: the pistol grip. I was anticipating, at most, a single sentence of additional detail. Instead, I received a quarter of an hour or so of precise instruction and informed discussion of the pros and cons, and when best to deploy the technique—the last few minutes, against the protests of all the other senior masters, who, by this time, were tired and hungry, and increasingly desperate to be allowed to go to dinner, but not without Professor Wally.

We became friends that day, for which I will be eternally grateful. Though he became friend and mentor to many, including Bruce Lee, those who can say that are not so many that it can ever be devalued. I'll never know what he saw in me. At the time I was *dan*-graded in around a dozen arts, and I had been teaching my own method for about seven years, and he seemed to enjoy our talks. We continued to correspond on a regular basis, and after about a year, I invited him to teach his first seminar in London. Shamefully, I had to cancel on him with a few months to spare, but he never held it against me; instead when Leon had a second wedding ceremony in London (having married a lovely English girl, Sandra, the previous year in California), he and Bernice stayed for a couple of weeks, and he dedicated that time to advancing my education.

Professor Wally expressed a wish to visit Scotland, so he, Bernice, and I took a train to Edinburgh. He dozed for most of the journey, but even when sleeping, he trained, performing his basic wrist extensions! At the end of that journey, I asked how such a gentle man (and he was a gentleman in every sense of the word) could spend pretty much every waking hour devising ever more painful ways to disable another human being? I was being only semi-serious, but he accepted this query in that grave, quiet way of his, and fell silent for several moments. Eventually he said, "I never thought of it that way; I guess I just think if you're going to do anything for a really long time, you should get more and more efficient, or why bother?"

I loved the way he thought. No question was out of bounds, and every part of one's performance was to be constantly reviewed critically. My own art, *Munen Muso Ryu* (School of No-Style, No Pre-Conception), wasn't any particular blend of the arts I had studied; it was a collection of principles and methodologies. I was not concerned with which version of say, *kote gaeshi* one used (although once I met the Professor, I naturally adopted the superior mechanics of Small Circle in applying any grappling technique I had learned). Finger-locking was a complete game-changer when it came to control and arrest techniques, especially as I had worked as a bodyguard (I know, if you've seen me, that will be hard to imagine) and later trained military, special forces, and law-enforcement personnel as close-protection operatives.

2

The Professor used to begin each seminar exactly the same way: He would ask for volunteers and then select the largest, youngest, fittest looking specimen among the black belts present. He would invite them to punch him. Naturally, they were usually reluctant to throw a full-power, full-speed punch at an elderly man, but until they did, he would just casually sway out of the path of the attack. After a while they got the idea that he really meant them to give him their best, but as soon as they began to raise their hands in earnest, Professor Wally would simply cup the elbow of the attacking arm as he pivoted off the center-line, and before they had raised their arms more than a few inches, he had secured their wrists and driven them nose-first into the mat with confrontation triceps tendon arm-bar!

These young, fit athletes—and everyone else watching—could scarcely believe just how fast he had taken control of his opponent (though really he was moving quite slowly, but with extraordinary economy of motion). He went on to demonstrate that same virtuoso skill and economy with every technique he taught, and, as a result, each time another dojo full of new believers was acquired…

—John Mellon, 7th Dan

CONVENTIONS

Because some of those featured in this work hold rank in many and varied systems, for the most part, only Small Circle Jujitsu rank is provided. Also, for clarity and simplicity, the Professors Jay (father and son) are typically referenced as either, "Professor Wally," or "Professor Leon," even though traditional convention would be to use, "Professor Jay." Finally, for grammatical accuracy, the pronouns "he" or "she" are used in conjunction with singular references to "the practitioner" and the like, but it should be understood that each is intended to embrace the other. With regard to these, and any other conventions employed in this work, nothing but respect is intended.

I. INTRODUCTION:
Gentleman, Gentle Way

When Peter Hobart, one of our fine Small Circle Black Belt instructors, first suggested writing this book together, I already knew that my father was a great man; highly respected and enormously talented. The process of gathering and reading the various contributions of his friends and colleagues—martial artists who knew him, trained with him and were influenced by him—has only served to further deepen my understanding of, and admiration and respect for him.

A sincere thank you to all who shared memories and experiences to create a true tribute to my father. My hope for this book is that it brings back many fond memories to those who were fortunate enough to know him, and for those that didn't have that privilege, that it serves as an example of what a true martial artist should be as a teacher and a human being.

My father had enormously high expectations of his children in the arts; expectations that weren't always easy to live up to. For a period of a few years as a young man, I found those very high standards he held us to pushed me in another direction, but his kindness, patience and perseverance pulled me back into the Small Circle fold, for which I will be forever grateful.

My father was an extraordinary innovator in the martial arts, and a positive influence and role model for many in the martial arts, both in their studies and their personal lives. He was one of those people who could gently guide you to that *eureka* moment in your personal journey, in and out of the martial arts. He had a typically Hawaiian way about him, whether telling corny jokes or discussing the deepest concepts of the martial arts, he was a very easy person to be with.

He never stopped seeking perfection; while touring with him, he often woke me up in the small hours to work on some insight that had come to him while asleep. Then, having worked through the latest insight from his sub-conscious, would go back to sleep, leaving me to try to calm myself enough to return to bed. Given the access his personal connections and the credibility that gave me to so many world-class martial artists, I really shouldn't complain!

Violence, in both the Hawaii he grew up in, and the mainland he moved to, was so prevalent, now and then, on the street and in the media, that it became his personal obsession to seek an effective way to de-escalate confrontations through compliance techniques. Blunt force trauma techniques are undoubtedly effective, but they can have unintended and unnecessary life-changing effects. Small Circle Jujitsu is the expression of his search for a bridge between the need for effective compliance techniques while offering the ethical option of doing so with little or no permanent injury.

Though Small Circle was designed primarily as a humane art for application in the civilian arena, it has been enthusiastically taken up by many law enforcement and military units for its sheer efficiency. At seminar tours it was always fun to watch my father in his later years easily control and subdue young and strong martial artists, often with only one finger— the skill and beauty of his art flowed from a kind and generous heart.

I believe that the memory of this exceptional man and martial artist deserves to be preserved; it has been my privilege to succeed him, and to continue his work with the many men and women of the Small Circle Jujitsu family, watching them all grow in the art, and I hope to do so for many years yet! I have not met my father's like, during his lifetime or since, and I doubt I ever will; but I do know his spirit lives on in his students and in theirs. *Aloha*, with love and thanks for hearing me, YS,

— Professor Leon Jay, 10th Dan, Headmaster of Small Circle Jujitsu

The first character in the word "*jujitsu*" is variously translated as: yielding, soft, or *gentle*. It is therefore entirely appropriate that one of the terms most commonly associated with Wally Jay is: "gentleman."

In fact, in the competitive, and sometimes cut-throat, community of the martial arts, it is impossible to find anyone with a bad thing to say about him! This reputation, standing alone, would be an amazing testament to the man. But his stellar character is always acknowledged in the same breath as his devastating power. And to find these two seemingly antithetical attributes in the same person is indeed a rare and valuable thing. Wally Jay could take you down in a heartbeat, and would do so with a kindly chuckle!

SHARING

The story is told of one of the famous 'triple seminars' in the 1980s at which Professor Wally was teaching in one room of a particular East Coast university, while two other grandmasters were conducting sessions in adjacent rooms. At some point, a well-meaning student burst into Professor Wally's room and reported to him that one of the other grandmasters had "stolen" his techniques and was teaching them in his own class!

Professor Wally simply smiled, and responded: *"Yes, I steal his techniques too—we call it 'sharing...'"*

During his martial arts career, Wally Jay came to be known as "the Professor." He held this title in both an athletic and an academic sense (being awarded an Honorary Doctorate by the College of Martial Arts in Sioux Falls, South Dakota, on May 4, 1991). But despite these high honors, any who met him can attest that he was among the most humble of men.

THE CHAIN

As martial artists, we each form an individual link in a chain of tradition that reaches back into the mists of antiquity and stretches forward over the horizon of the future. Each successive generation passes the torch of knowledge along to the next.

A wise master once said that he who writes the book gets to ask the questions. The answers to those questions can often unlock the secrets of the arts. In this regard, those who experienced first-hand the heady days when the Eastern fighting arts first arrived on Western shores truly hold the keys...

SMALL CIRCLE JUJITSU

·◊· LINDA LEE-CADWELL ·◊·

The Lee and the Jay families were always very close to one another. From the early days, the Jays took us in and made us welcome. I knew and liked Bernice very much, and have met Leon many times over the years.

Professor Wally Jay was always one of our favorite people—a perfect gentleman, always so courteous, emanating love for other people. In fact, I have never met anyone in the martial arts community who has a bad thing to say about him, which is a pretty remarkable achievement! He always showed such care for others, 'looking straight across' at them, never 'looking down' on them.

At the same time, Wally could back up his reputation on the mat. Bruce [Lee] always had great respect for Wally's abilities, as well as for his thought processes. Small Circle Jujitsu undoubtedly had an influence on Bruce. Bruce was always exploring; always looking for a better way (especially after the famous fight with Wong Jack Man), and certainly Professor Wally's art of Small Circle Jujitsu added to Bruce's research and education. In addition, some martial artists claim to take credit for teaching Bruce this or that, but Professor Wally never did.

To Leon,
There is a
strong bond
between the
Jay family and
the Lee family.
Let's keep it
that way.
Love,
Linda Lee

Wally was over twenty years older than Bruce, and in that way, they had a kind of uncle-nephew relationship. In some ways, Bruce looked up to Wally as a mentor, but at the same time, they also regarded each other as being on equal footing. They 'looked straight across' at each other in this way. In fact, this is a trait that Wally and Bruce both had in common: Never looking down on someone as a result of age, ethnicity, gender, experience etc... I think this is one of the reasons they became such good friends. They respected each other's abilities and they both viewed martial arts—and the value of it in this world—in the same way...

—Linda Lee-Cadwell

Wally,
my
best to
you
Bruce Lee

For those who are new to the art of Small Circle Jujitsu, this work is intended to whet the appetite, to help to navigate the way forward, and to document the journey. For those who are already familiar with this system, it is hoped that it may nonetheless provide a few interesting tidbits to chew on, as well as a thoughtful stroll down memory lane...

II. THE FOUNDER:

Professor Wally

On June 15, 1917, Wah Leong "Wally" Jay was born in Honolulu, Hawaii, to Albert Yat Jay and Tim Chang. He was the third child in what was to be a line of six (Mew Quon Ho, Mew Yung Chu, Alfred Jay, Elsie Sniffen, and John Jay).

Wally was a somewhat frail child. In an effort to help build his strength and confidence, he began studying boxing under Jimmy Mitchell at the age of eleven. By the time he turned eighteen he was studying jujitsu under Paul Kaelemakule.

In 1938, Wally enrolled at Oregon State College, where he studied, among other things, medicine and agriculture. He also resumed his boxing career here under the tutelage of coach Jim Dixon. By 1940, he had returned to Hawaii, where he began studying *Danzan Ryu Jujitsu* under Juan Gomez, a fifth degree black belt and one of the senior students of the system's founder, Henry Seishiro Okazaki. During this same time, he also began training in judo with Hawaiian champion Ken Kawachi.

Wally married his wife Bernice in 1941. In 1944, Wally earned his first black belt in Danzan Ryu. In 1945, he received certification in restorative massage from the Nikko Restoration Massage Institute in Honolulu. The husband-wife team went on to study martial arts and massage therapy together, and in 1948, they were both awarded certificates of mastery (*menkyo kaiden*) by Professor Okazaki.

In 1950, Wally and Bernice moved to Alameda, California, where they built a small gym behind their house (the birthplace of the Island Judo Jujitsu Club).

Here, the Professor trained many local, state, and national champions, and by the early 1960s, he had earned his third degree black belt in judo, and been named Coach of the Year by the *Hokka Judo Yudanshakai*. In 1962, the Professor first met Bruce Lee. The two were to become fast friends and frequent training partners over the years that followed. Throughout that decade and the next, the Professor coached competitive fighting teams that toured the Americas.

·◊· WILLY "CLIPPER" CAHILL ·◊·

I was born in Hawaii in 1935. My father [John Cahill Senior] and Wally Jay were both students of Professor Henry Okazaki [the founder of Danzan Ryu Jujitsu]. As a child, I suffered from polio, and the doctors told my father that I might never be able to walk, but Professor Okazaki—who was also a healer—gave me therapeutic leg massages regularly, and we proved the doctors wrong! After that, I continued to study with Professor Okazaki until my family moved to California in 1947.

We opened a judo school in Daly City and later in some other places (San Francisco, San Mateo). We had a lot of success. Our teams competed in the California State Judo Championships and the United States Judo Association Championships, and won all the time—the only time we lost was to Stanford: My old team! I went on to coach teams that competed in the Olympics, the Goodwill Games, and the World Judo Championships [Professor Cahill was named Judo Instructor of the Year in the Black Belt Hall of Fame in 1975].

> ### FOCUS
>
> Focus is the key. Wally and I both stress the importance of mental focus. Once you get your students to focus—especially the young ones—they will start to get it. It doesn't matter what you are saying if no-one is listening. Once the bell rings, playtime is over!

It was in California that I connected with Wally. My father was at his place in Alameda for a seminar in the early days and introduced me to him. I had heard of him as a child in Hawaii, where he was one of the most well-known martial arts masters. After that, we trained together all the time and went on to found Jujitsu America with some other martial artist in 1978.

> ### THE POWER OF THE WRIST
>
> One of the most amazing things about Wally was how he could control you using just a wrist lock, no matter who you were. He had amazing control, and a lot of it was in the wrist. He had such a supple wrist! After he grabbed you by the lapel and sleeve, he would snap his wrists—pull with one and push with the other in one motion—and get you going in the direction he wanted. He would shake guys up with that little move, and get the [automatic] reaction he wanted. It starts with the little finger and you dig your knuckles into the other guy's body. That is an important thing I learned from Wally Jay.

In 1994, Wally promoted me to 10th Degree in jujitsu [Professor Cahill is also a 9th Degree Black Belt in judo].

○ In 1964, Professor Wally won the AJI Outstanding Coach Award;

○ In 1968, a student of the Professor's—David Quinonez—won the National High School Judo Championship 120 Pound Crown;

○ In 1969, the Professor was inducted into the *Black Belt* Hall of Fame for his contributions to the art of judo;

○ In 1970, another student of the Professor's—Bradford Burgo—won the National High School Judo Championship 120 Pound Crown;

○ In 1972, the Professor retired from the U.S. Postal Service and went back to school, eventually earning his B.A. from Sonoma State College;

○ In 1977, the Professor and various colleagues founded Jujitsu America;

○ In 1980, the Professor was inducted into the *Black Belt* Hall of Fame for his contributions to the art of jujitsu;

○ In 1985, the Professor was the first person to be invited to captain an American team at the International Wushu Championship in Xian, China;

○ In 1990, the Professor was named *Black Belt's* Man of the Year;

○ In 1991, the Professor was awarded an Honorary Doctorate by the College of Martial Arts in Sioux Falls, South Dakota;

○ In 1992, the Professor was invited to demonstrate his art at Japan's *Dai Nippon Butokuden*;

○ In 1993, the Professor was inducted into the Danzan Ryu Hall of Fame;

○ In 1999, the Professor was named on *Inside Kung Fu's* Most Influential Martial Artists List;

○ In 2002, the Professor officially designated his son, Leon, as the new Headmaster of Small Circle Jujitsu;

• On May 29, 2011, at the age of ninety-three, Professor Wally Jay joined the ranks of the past masters, survived by his wife Bernice, his children, Alberta, Alan, Antoinette, Leon, and Winona (hanai'd), fifteen grandchildren, six great-grandchildren, scores of nieces and nephews, and thousands of friends and students all over the world...

III. HISTORY OF THE ART:
Danzan Ryu

The Japanese combat techniques of jujitsu (also rendered "jujutsu" or "jiu-jitsu") date back approximately 2000 years. The exact origins of the art are unclear as most of its history has been passed down through the oral tradition. The few early written references to this art indicate that it dates back to mythological times.

Jujitsu was formalized and popularized during the Edo period in Japan. This was a time when the *samurai* caste dominated Japanese life and culture. Should he be unable to access his swords for any reason, jujitsu was the samurai's primary system of self-defense, and indeed many of the system's techniques are derived from the motion of the *katana*. There have been many schools (*ryu*) of jujitsu throughout history in Japan, and during the Twentieth Century, many more styles were developed all over the world.

Small Circle Jujitsu is based on this ancient classical jujitsu, but its real evolution dates back to the 1940s, when Professor Wally Jay studied *Kodenkan Jujitsu* under Professor Henry Okazaki in Hawaii. Professor Okazaki had himself been a student of several classical jujitsu systems— *Yoshin Ryu*, *Kosagabe Ryu*, and *Iwaga Ryu*—as well as Okinawan *karate*, Filipino knife fighting, Hawaiian *lua*, the Spanish art dirk-throwing, Western boxing, wrestling and Chinese *kung fu*. Professor Okazaki was something of a rebel, and broke from tradition on many occasions, developing his own style of jujitsu (Kodenkan), and teaching his art to non-Japanese, which was unheard of at the time.

In 1944, Professor Jay received his black belt in Kodenkan Danzan Ryu Jujitsu from Professor Okazaki.

By the time Professor Jay became a student of Professor Okazaki, he had already studied boxing, weightlifting, judo, and jujitsu with various other instructors. He had always felt that there was something missing from jujitsu the way he originally learned it. His prior experiences, together with Okazaki's multi-disciplinary background, gave him the perspective he needed to see how classical jujitsu could be improved.

It was, however, the years he spent cross-training in judo with Ken Kawachi that gave Professor Jay the key to Small Circle Jujitsu. When he was taking his blue belt exam (in Kodenkan Jujitsu), there was one particular throw that gave him real difficulty. Unhappy with his own performance, he had decided to refuse this promotion. Kawachi Sensei, however, advised him to accept it, promising that he would teach him how to master the throw.

Kawachi Sensei—a physically diminutive man—was the Hawaiian judo champion for many years. The secret to his success was that he stressed the use of the wrist action to gain superior leverage, and so effective was he in exploiting the subtleties of the grip that he routinely dominated other *judoka* literally twice his size, and defeated many contenders from the islands as well as the mainland. It was this same **wrist action** that became the key to Small Circle Jujitsu. And over the years that followed, Professor Wally made many other radical changes to the classical jujitsu techniques he had learned, believing that this was what his teacher, Professor Okazaki, would have wanted.

Professor Jay's years of experience in classical jujitsu, judo, boxing, weightlifting, wrestling, aikido, kung fu, other martial arts, and many years of trial and error, led him to develop his own, unique approach to combat, which he originally called **Small Circle Theory**. His goal was to refine and improve upon the original techniques by combining the best of everything he had learned in these different disciplines. **Small Circle Theory** was rapidly accepted by the martial arts community at large, and was soon recognized as an acclaimed and accredited system.

Small Circle Theory is applicable not only to jujitsu, but also to many other styles of martial arts. When Professor Wally first began coaching judo, for example, his teams did not fare well and he was mocked by some of his peers. In typical Wally Jay fashion, this experience simply made him all the more determined to prove the efficacy of his methods. When he began to apply **Small Circle Theory** to his judo teaching, his students began winning competition after competition. In 1960, he was voted Northern California Judo Coach of the Year, and throughout the 1960s and 1970s, he produced national champions and winning teams in the USA, Canada, and Mexico.

In 1978, Professor Jay, Willy Cahill, John Chow-Hoon, and Carl Beaver created a new association—**Jujitsu America**—intended to represent the mainland-based teachers who had broken away from the island-based traditions in which they had initially been indoctrinated. They seceded from the Hawaii-based American Jujitsu Institute because of conflicting ideologies and methodologies: The Hawaiian leaders were intent on perpetuating the traditions of the Kodenkan system, while the state-siders, being modernists, wanted to update and improve their fighting skills to reflect certain modern realities.

Following this break, **Small Circle Theory** continued to improve and evolve until 1987, when it was officially recognized as a complete style of its own (**Small Circle Jujitsu**). While many already recognized the Small Circle system prior to this time, following the publication of an article in *Black Belt* magazine to this effect, it became widely and officially recognized.

The techniques of Small Circle Jujitsu are smooth and functional because of Professor Jay's mastery of what he came to call '**transitional flow**'—one of the key principles of the system. It is in this regard that Professor Jay's in-depth study of body mechanics allowed him to move smoothly and economically from one technique to the next in order to counter any moves by an attacker.

In August 2002, Professor Wally Jay held a ceremony officially handing the title of Grandmaster over to his son, Professor Leon Jay, in his hometown of Alameda, California, near San Francisco. Since that time, **Small Circle Jujitsu**, which arose from many sources and elements, has continued to evolve as Professor Leon Jay and others enhance the style with their knowledge.

○ **Small Circle Practice Pointer:** Small Circle Jujitsu is an evolving art.

IV. THE USERS GUIDE:
Checklist & Manual

The principles of Small Circle Jujitsu can be used as both a checklist and a manual:

Checklist: As Professor Leon often says, *"When performing a technique, ask yourself, 'Am I on balance? Should I be mobile or stable? Am I avoiding head-on collision of forces...'"* By working through this list, the Small Circle practitioner can ensure that the effectiveness of every technique is maximized.

> o **Small Circle Practice Pointer:** For every technique you practice, ask yourself: 'Am I balanced; do I need mobility or stability here; am I avoiding head-on collisions; etc...'

Technically speaking, there may be some overlap among the principles from time-to-time. For example, there is frequently some conceptual common ground when considering the interplay between **two-way action** and **fulcrum-lever-base**, but in practice, each is sufficiently different from an operational point-of-view to warrant its own category.

Manual: Early on in the Small Circle practitioner's education, the following question is presented: *"How do you deal with an opponent with high pain tolerance?"* While Small Circle Principles provide a helpful guide for improving the effectiveness of <u>any</u> technique, they also serve as a manual for solving any problem relating to the application of a <u>specific</u> technique.

For instance, when confronted with an opponent who is resistant to arm-locks, **energy transfer** may be the solution. And if strikes to the target are failing to produce the desired effect, **focusing to the smallest point** or taking advantage of the **cascade effect** may solve the problem.

○ **Small Circle Practice Pointer:** If a technique is not working, run through the list of principles to determine how the effect can be amplified.

And, as you advance in your Small Circle training, you may start to find that some of the most helpful words in your "manual" are those that you yourself write there…

V. PRINCIPLES & PRECEPTS:
The Heart of the Art

In creating and refining the art of Small Circle Jujitsu, Professor Wally Jay developed ten guiding principles, each of which resonates with well-established western scientific precepts across a variety of disciplines (for more on this, *see* Appendix A).

The first of these Principles is: **Balance**…

·◊· DAVID RHODES ·◊·

It has been theorized that all humans are 'balance savants'; that is, we possess the extraordinary ability to stay constantly balanced, whether we are standing (static balance) or in motion (dynamic balance). The next time you slip on a sheet of ice or a slippery floor, however, you may disagree with the idea that we are all masters of balance.

As with art, we all know good balance when we see it. There are a lot of definitions of balance, so I took several of them and combined them into the following: Balance is the ability of a person to stay upright and steady while remaining in control of body movement by maintaining center-of-gravity above, and within, the base of support, producing an even distribution of weight, minimal postural sway, and physical equilibrium, creating the ability to neutralize forces that might disturb that equilibrium so that they do not fall.

No wonder we sometimes have a hard time staying balanced with all of that maintaining, producing, distribution and creating! But we *do* stay in balance and it is because we have many genetic abilities that specifically help us to be 'balance savants'. Our bodies are arranged from head to toe to form an upright 'antigravity pole'. Additionally, our eyes, inner ears, vestibulocochlear nerves, cerebellum, proprioception (the ability to determine the position of our body parts relative to one another), joints, and muscles all work together to keep us from losing our balance.

When we slip or trip, our bodies start to become unbalanced in just a few milliseconds. Since it takes the brain longer than this to decide how to keep us in balance, our bodies use reflex arcs. A reflex arc allows nerves to skip past the brain and activate spinal reflex actions that transmit messages directly to the correct muscles for balance corrections. Spinal reflex actions produce nearly instantaneous movements in response to stimuli and do not require any conscious thought. Some reflexes that keep us 'in balance' include:

o Postural Reflex—Keeps the body upright and aligned;

o Righting Reflex—Helps the body respond to rapid loss of balance;

o Stretch Reflex (Reciprocal Inhibition)—Contracts muscle in response to stretching;

o Equilibrium Reactions—Alters the position/size of the body base.

As Professor Wally Jay points out in his book, <u>Small Circle Jujitsu</u> (O'Hara, 1989): "Balance is perhaps the most important principle in any sport." Good balance promotes kinesthetic awareness (knowing where your body is in all three dimensions) so we can move smoothly and confidently. Maintaining balance allows us to be strong, agile, and focused; to react more quickly; to think more clearly; to shift our center of gravity up, down, and outside of our base; all the while providing a strong sense of where our body is in relation to the things around us so we suffer fewer injuries. Being 'in balance' allows us to move in all directions, change stances, punch, kick, grab, push, pull, throw, perform takedowns, fall, roll, and get back up. It allows us to employ the other principles of Small Circle Jujitsu.

With poor balance, a person is more prone to falls, decreased spinal mobility, and slower reflexes. Since these are the traits we want an *attacker* to have, we need *our* techniques to emphasize balance destruction. If you think that you'll just punch your opponents in the head, remember that if they still have balance, they will block your punch or simply avoid it, and then be able to counter-attack from a balanced position of strength. All of this means that we have to maintain *our* balance while we take our *opponents'* balance away, so they can't punch, kick, grab, push, pull, throw, and perform takedowns on us. Then—and just as important—we must *keep* them off balance and under control.

If you ever saw Professor Wally Jay, or have seen Professor Leon Jay, performing techniques, picture what their ukes look like during a demonstration: Hands flying in the air; arms reaching out to the side or in front of them; legs bent; bodies bending forward or backward; upper torsos twisting in different directions; lying on the mat in the fetal position, in a pretzel or… Well, you get the picture. None of their ukes stay in balance.

But what about all those reflexes that keep our opponents' bodies in balance? No problem. We use techniques that trigger *other* spinal reflex actions that we can use against them.

o Withdrawal Reflex—The body pulls away from pain;

o Stretch Reflex (Reciprocal Inhibition)—Contracts muscle in response to stretching;

o Golgi Tendon Reflex—Causes muscle relaxation before force can tear a tendon;

o Crossed Extensor Reflex—When muscles on one side of the body engage in withdrawal reflex, contracts the muscles on the other side to help keep the body in balance;

o Startle Reflex—Reacts to perceived danger to help you get away/defend yourself (think flinching).

There are many ways to take advantage of these reflexes. Some options include:

- Body Weight—Pounce on them! Every guy bigger than you knows this one;

- Tackling—Works on any given Sunday in the U.S.;

- Strength—If you can bench press your attacker, why not?

- Slap the Eyes/Ears—Two important areas that help maintain balance;

- Distractions—Start getting your attacker into their reflexes;

- Pain—As Professor Wally always said: "Pain makes believers!"

- Blending—When they push, you pull. When they pull, you push. That is the definition of jujitsu;

- Pressure Points—Bend joints, create pain, stun or knock them out;

- Locks, Wraps and Bars—Might as well put your training to good use!

- Forward Pressure—Keep your opponent off balance;

- Center Line Concentration—Focus pressure to the center of the opponents' bodies;

- Rotational Momentum—Keep your opponents' base moving so they can't recover their balance;

- Long Bone Guide—The skeleton points the way to the ground;

- *Kuzushi* Triangle Point—Know where to drop the opponent for optimal control;

- Short, loud instructions—When in pain, people are open to suggestions (think of Wally Jay's "up, up, up!").

LONG BONE GUIDE

If you reduce the human body to a stick-man drawing, the "long bones" would be the femur (long bone of the leg) and the humerus (long bone of the arm). I have found that when doing technique, these "long bones" often aim perfectly toward the kuzushi point. When a technique causes your opponent to bend his knees, the femur points in the right direction to take him down. When applying a wrist lock, the humerus (or sometimes the radius) will do the same. If your opponent is bent sideways, imagine a line from shoulder to shoulder; just push or pull along this line and they will fall...

You can combine two or more of these together to make it easier to take the opponent out of balance. For example, distract an attacker causing them to flinch away and follow up with sticking control and sensitivity and forward pressure to blend with them as they throw an arm or hand up to try and maintain balance. This creates the opportunity for you to get a lock and, with continuing forward pressure, drop them to a kuzushi triangle point.

Once the attacker has been controlled, you must continue to control their balance until the incident is finished. Remember, Professor Wally Jay said many times that Small Circle Jujitsu is primarily for controlling an attacker. As he wrote in chapter four of <u>Small Circle Jujitsu</u>: "Using a minimum of force is important because joint locks can be extremely damaging and you do not want to go beyond what is necessary to subdue and restrain your assailant." Just because a person does something stupid does not mean they should never be able to use their arm again. So, this might mean you should maintain control of the attacker until friends step in to help or someone calls the police.

But, in some instances, you may have had to incapacitate the attacker with an injury or knockout. As Professor Wally Jay also pointed out: "When attacked, there are times when you must hurt your attacker to the point of painful dislocation. If this must be done to save yourself, do not hesitate."

Some advanced balance control options include:

o Pulsing the lock/point so the attacker cannot fight through the pain;

o Changing the angle of the lock to force the attacker to constantly adjust their balance;

o Maintaining forward pressure which keeps the attacker worried about maintaining balance.

So why do we still see students who are not taking their training partners out of balance? When we get stressed, we get tense. When we get tense, our muscles contract so that they can respond quickly for protection. Our heart rate goes up to rush blood to the muscles to help prevent injury (and there are over a thousand muscles in the human body). When we encounter resistance, our muscles get ready for action, so we usually go to strength solutions first and forget our techniques. Students start grappling with their opponents, which makes the attack last longer, which, in turn, results in students getting tired quicker and losing their strength and mobility.

When students first learn a new technique, it is stored in their short-term memory, which is an *electrical* activity. As they become better at performing the technique, they become smoother and more fluid and their technical ability moves into their long-term memory, which is a *chemical* process. Their technique then becomes instinctive and they begin to understand why balance destruction is important for all other techniques.

The solution is to teach, and then constantly train and reinforce correct balance destruction and balance control so that they become instinctive. To achieve this instructors should:

○ Demonstrate new techniques slowly and several times;

○ Break complicated techniques down into sections and demonstrate each section slowly;

○ Show how the technique takes away the opponent's balance and does not allow them to regain it;

○ Structure practice so that the student goes slowly, does the move correctly, and receives immediate, positive feedback for being able to execute the technique successfully; and

○ Give the student time to practice the technique and reinforce with periodic training of the technique.

Only then will it all imprint into their long-term memory and become instinctive!

—David Rhodes, 6th Dan

THE ORIGINAL TEN PRINCIPLES

1. **Balance:** Center-of-gravity over base [*physics*].

2. **Mobility and Stability:** Changing center-of-gravity [*physics*].

3. **Avoid Head-on Collision of Forces:** $F=m(\Delta v/\Delta t)$ [*physics*].

4. **Mental Resistance and Distraction:** Hypoalgesia [*neurology*].

5. **Focus to Smallest Point:** $P=f/a$ [*physics*].

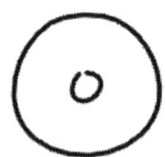

6. **Energy Transfer**: Hyperalgesia [*neurology*].

7. **Fulcrum, Lever, and Base**: $F_e = (F_l \times d_l)/d_e$ [*physics*].

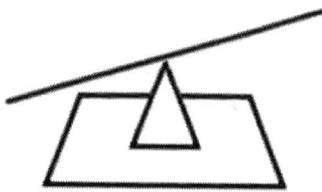

8. **Sticking, Control, and Sensitivity**: Reflex arcs [*neurology*].

9. **Rotational Momentum**: Antagonistic muscles [*biomechanics*].
   (Spiral Motion: Exponential reduction [*mathematics*]).

10. **Transitional Flow**: Operant conditioning [*psychology*].

Transitional flow is in many ways the culmination of all other principles. Like Professor Wally's "Dance of Pain," it showcases all of the practitioner's skills and abilities working together, and is a great litmus test for the student's level of proficiency. In some ways, it is the "kata" of Small Circle Jujitsu...

These Ten Principles are well known to Small Circle practitioners the world over, and their scientific underpinnings are discussed in detail in Appendix A to this work.

But, as noted martial arts master Leo Fong explains, *"An art that does not grow and evolve becomes stagnant."* According to Master Fong, if any of the great past masters were to return to the world today and find their art unchanged, they would be sorely disappointed.

MARTIAL GIANTS

My family was very fond of Leo Fong. My parents were so impressed that he was a martial artist and a minister. He was also a close friend of Bruce Lee. He wrote several books on kung fu, including Choy Lay Fut and Sil Lum. He is another martial arts icon, and we should be grateful that he came into this world.

—Guro Dan Inosanto

Jujitsu is a martial art that is rooted in antiquity. Its techniques have been battle-tested in the crucible of time. The efficacy and reliability of foundational moves like the arm-bar and the hip throw, for example, have been established in close quarters combat, in a wide variety of contexts, over the centuries. Their provenance is well established.

But for a martial art to truly thrive, the roots from which it sprang should feed living, growing branches. That is to say, it is natural, and indeed beneficial, for the art to evolve over time. For example, the *Tanju no Maki* of Professor Okazaki's *Danzan Ryu* contains defenses from a handgun—a weapon that came into existence long after the fundamentals of this classical jujitsu system had been established.

The Small Circle system has both strong roots and thriving branches. It is a living art. As a result, modifications may be made from time-to-time to reflect the changing tactical, ethical, and legal imperatives of modern society. One example of this kind of 'pruning' at play is the shift toward neck restraints as an alternative to the far more dangerous chokes and strangles. Another is the decision made by Second Generation Headmaster Leon Jay and his senior instructors that the time has come to recognize certain aspects of the art as **Principles** in their own right:

THE NEW PRINCIPLES

11. **Two-way Action:** Anyone who has trained in Small Circle Jujitsu for any length of time knows that **two-way action**—together with the **wrist snap**—is embedded in the very fabric of the art. There are many possible reasons that these were not originally identified as "Principles"—including the fact that they overlap to some degree with existing pillars of the system, such as **fulcrum-lever-base** and **energy transfer**—but they are now!

12. **Wrist Snap:** Professor Wally always credited Sensei Ken Kawachi with imparting this bedrock principle to him when the two trained together on the judo mat.

13. **Pulsing and Waving:** Altering the intensity and direction of the force being applied in any given technique can have a dramatic effect on the result, overcoming virtually any kind of resistance.

14. **The Cascade Effect:** This well-documented natural law speaks to the power of accelerating an effect by 'stacking' multiple stimuli, and can be seen at play in such fields as fluid dynamics and pain management.

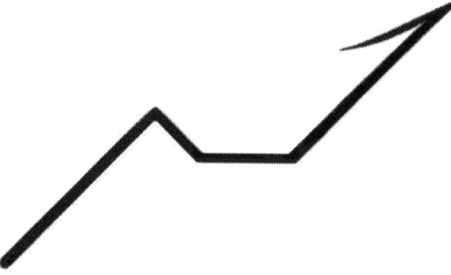

15. **Whiplash Strikes:** Sometimes described as 'the push-pull principle,' this modified striking method dramatically increases the impact of a blow in much the same way that snapping a bull whip accelerates a hand movement of perhaps a hundred miles an hour to twice the speed of sound.

16. **Entries & Exits:** While these concepts are not, strictly speaking, part of any particular throw, lock, or grapple, they bookend existing techniques beautifully and to devastating effect!

○ **Small Circle Practice Pointer:** Study the *sixteen* principles!

VI. TWO-WAY ACTION:
"The Eleventh Principle"

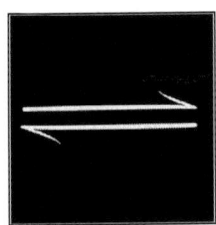

There are several martial traditions for passing along teachings in a subtle manner. One is *kuden*—the oral tradition—where certain secrets (*oku*) are never to be committed to writing. Another is hiding the message in plain sight—in which the lesson is placed right in front of the world for any who have eyes to see it. This may take the form of the name of a *kata*, a line on a certificate, or a symbol on an emblem.

In the case of Small Circle Jujitsu, there are only a few elements to the patch: The kanji for the "Jay" family name (which is loosely translated as "friendship"); the tapered belt looped in an infinity shape, symbolizing an ever-tightening focus and the seamlessness of the flow; and the twin arcing arrows, which symbolize the core concept of **two-way action**.

Two-way action is a foundational principle of Professor Jay's art and was one of the primary breakthroughs that caused Small Circle theory to evolve into a separate system of its own. Its effect can be seen in virtually every technique in the syllabus of the art (*see* Appendix B), from taking **balance** (e.g., *o soto gari*) to **energy transfer** (e.g., *ude osae*), but nowhere is this principle more clearly at play than in the physics of **fulcrum, lever, and base**. And perhaps it is this very foundational pervasiveness that caused **two-way action** not to be included in the original list of principles—until now...

The essential idea underlying this bedrock concept is that instead of moving the target (a limb, a joint, even an entire body) by simply manipulating it in *one* direction, the Small Circle practitioner uses (at least) *two*. By pushing in one place, for instance, while at the same time pulling in another, the effect of any given technique can be vastly increased.

The power of **two-way action** can perhaps be most easily understood in the context of a simple lever system where force (↓) is applied to a lever arm (—) that is resting on a fulcrum (Δ), in order to move a load (○).

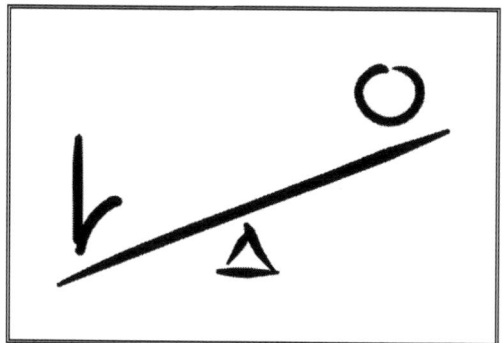

A fulcrum is often defined in physics as, "a fixed point around which a lever rotates," the key word being "fixed". If the fulcrum is unstable, the lever will not work. Imagine, for example, trying to lift a heavy object with a lever whose fulcrum was floating on quicksand. Intuitively, we know that this would not work—the fulcrum would simply be pressed down into the quicksand—and scientific testing by attempting to apply lever action on a yielding surface confirms the validity of this instinctive response.

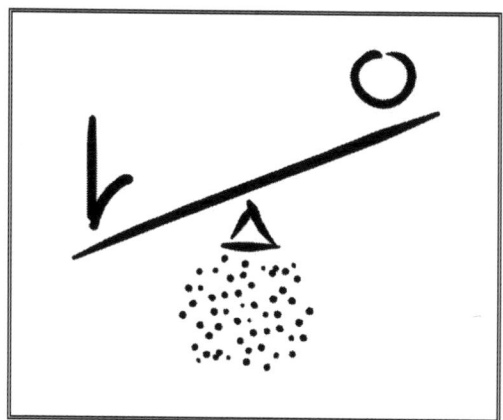

Now, if we were to place a board, or some other form of stabilization (a **base**) underneath the fulcrum, the result changes, and the effort moves the load much more easily.

But if instead of merely supporting the fulcrum, we were to *raise* it at the same time that we *depress* the lever, the result changes again, this time, dramatically amplifying the power of the mechanism.

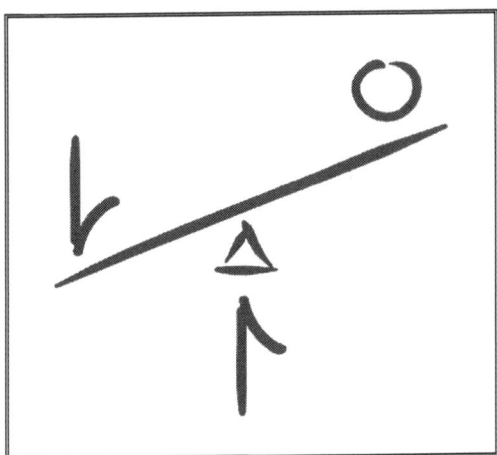

This is the power of **two-way action!** And once mastered, it can be applied in almost every technique in the Small Circle curriculum.

> ○ **Small Circle Practice Pointer:** It is important to keep in mind that there is a critical distinction between *mechanical* levers and *martial* levers. The objective of the *mechanical* lever is to move the load at the other end, whereas the goal in the *martial* realm is to break—or threaten to break—the lever itself! Thus, while the mechanical principles are the same, the method of application can be quite different...

Two-Way Action—Selected Applications

1. **Locks**: For example, using the basic index finger lock as a model, many arts teach the student to bend that digit against the joint merely by applying *backwards* pressure, but the Small Circle practitioner knows that the effect of this technique can be increased exponentially by applying *forward* pressure to the base of the finger at the same time, thus creating **two-way action**.

2. **Throws**: All throws benefit greatly from the application of force in at least two complimentary directions, but nowhere is this more apparent—and indeed necessary—as *tenchi nage*, the heaven-and-earth throw. By pulling down on the opponent's right arm while simultaneously pushing up on his left, the Small Circle practitioner can throw his adversary quite easily.

3. **Neck Restraints/Escapes**: Even neck restraints, which tend to work quite well with only 'one-way action,' can be drastically improved by adding a second angle of attack. Consider *hadaka jime*, the rear interlocking neck restraint, for example: By applying pressure to the carotid artery from two sides simultaneously, the opponent can be subdued almost instantaneously.

4. **Strikes**: Even when striking, the Small Circle practitioner can take advantage of the power of **two-way action**. By pulling the opponent toward the strike, for example, or even tricking him into advancing into the technique, the practitioner can amplify the power of her forward momentum with that of the opponent.

5. **Strategy**: And as with any principle of true value, the mechanical lessons of **two-way action** can be applied in a strategic manner as well. How many times in history have wise generals enticed the enemy to advance with vigor right into the jaws of a pincer maneuver, effectively using the opposing army's momentum against it? This is the power of **two-way action** at play on the strategic level...

SMALL CIRCLE EXERCISE—WRIST EXTENSIONS

Mastering the movements contained in the wrist extension exercises—the first drill that most Small Circle students learn—will make the application of **two-way action** instinctive.

VII. WRIST SNAP:
"The Twelfth Principle"

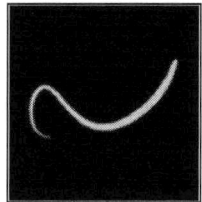

> Both have feathers and fly through the air, but a sparrow is not an arrow!
>
> —Philosopher's axiom

The principles of Small Circle Jujitsu fit together like finely dovetailed woodwork, each blending seamlessly with the adjacent pieces. As a result, there will be times when their characteristics merge or overlap with one another to a degree. This does not mean that they are redundant. Rather, each is intended to focus the practitioner on a discrete concept that will amplify the performance of any technique. By way of example: An axe and a lathe are both edged metal tools designed to cut wood, but each serves a very different purpose. It may be helpful to keep this differentiation in mind when analyzing and compartmentalizing the principles of this art.

Like the crack of the whip's tip or the blast of an explosive round on impact, the **wrist snap** adds some extra power to the distal end of any arm-based technique. Professor Wally credits Hawaiian Judo champion Ken Kawachi with teaching him the power of the **wrist snap**. It was while the Professor was trying to master a particular throw that the diminutive Kawachi first showed him how minor motions of the wrist could be used to gain superior leverage over much larger opponents.

KAWACHI SENSEI

Ken Kawachi was one of Hawaii's judo Grand Champions who held the title for several years in a row against much larger opponents despite being small in stature. Kawachi Sensei had great wrist control and was able to manage opponents with his firm grip and its rotating action. Professor Wally Jay would often remind us how important wrist action was to our judo, citing Ken Kawachi's prowess, so much so that he would have us practice several different motions, flexing and retracting our wrists, to ingrain in them specific motions, cultivating our "muscle memory" for eventual instinctive use later on. Many of these I still practice and instruct my own students to do in my current judo and jujitsu classes. Movements like vertical, horizontal, and rotational wrist extensions and retractions, thumb-wrist entry, and hand-wrist radius exercises, have all proven their usefulness throughout my judo career, as well as within my Small Circle Jujitsu teaching and applications.

—Dave Quinonez, 7th Dan

GRIPPING UP AND THE WALK-AROUND-SLOWLY DANCE

Anyone who has witnessed a playground scuffle or a less-than-earnest street-fight will be familiar with what is sometimes referred to as, "the walk around slowly dance." In this kind of engagement, two would-be combatants grab hold of each other—usually by some part of the jacket, or, for some, the hair—and wrestle each other in a perpetual circle, occasionally freeing up one of the gripping hands to fire off a lackluster strike here or there.

In much the same way that bite inhibition allows wolves from the same pack to battle for dominance without inflicting serious damage on one another, this cross-cultural instinct in humans allows rivals to try their strength without risking the kind of lasting injuries (like brain-damage or disfigurement) that repeated blows to the head can often cause. It sets up a contest in which the fighters can make brief forays into the dangerous and unpredictable world of striking, before retreating back into the relative safety and stability of the wrestler's hold.

And given this combination of relative safety of execution and commonness of occurrence, this position is an excellent pad from which to launch a variety of Small Circle techniques. The 'gripped-up' position is taken by having each combatant grab the other's *left* lapel with his *right* hand, and the opponent's *right* sleeve with his *left* hand. And while at first glance each 'gripped-up' fighter appears to be a mirror image of the other, subtle differences in the position and angle of the hands can make all the difference when push quite literally comes to shove!

SMALL CIRCLE EXERCISE—GRIPPING UP

To make sure that the 'lapel hand' has a firm grip that is capable of controlling the opponent, practice by having him lie supine on the floor and using that grip to elevate his torso, like hauling up a sack of potatoes! Also, once gripped up this way, the practitioner can lever the index knuckle into LU-1 by simply performing a forward wrist extension.

To make sure that the 'sleeve hand' has a firm grip that is capable of moving the opponent, practice by having him try to strike your open (right) palm with his (dominant) right hand while 'gripped up' at his right elbow. Not only will this mid-point tether thwart his attempts to land any kind of meaningful strike; if the practitioner twists the sleeve with a rotating inward wrist extension, he may be able to exert pain and choke off blood supply depending on the girth of the opponent's arm and the size of his gi. This inward twist on the left—especially in combination with a forward extension on the right—will also dramatically enhance kuzushi.

A vital part of 'gripping up' for the Small Circle practitioner is making sure to position himself in preparation for the application of **wrist snaps** in conjunction with the larger arm movements involved in the off-balancing aspects of any given technique. These 'snaps' assist with the execution of technique in at least three different ways:

1. **Extension—'Snap':** Just as the final extension of the fist at the moment of impact when punching helps the weapon to reach and penetrate its target, a snap of the wrist can increase the arc and strength of an off-balancing or redirecting push or pull;

2. **Shock—'Pop':** In addition, the 'pop' of a powerful **wrist snap** is sudden and jarring, so it tends to shock the recipient's nervous system far more than would the gradual application of pressure that typically accompanies a push or pull that is entirely arm-based;

3. **Compounding—'Crack':** Finally, the wrist can be rotated in a variety of directions and need not follow the basic trajectory of the arm-based portion of the technique. In this way, the practitioner can exploit the fact that it is virtually impossible to resist in two directions at the same time. Instead of merely breaking balance to the back-left corner in setting up O Soto Gari, for instance, he can simultaneously rotate the opponent counter-clockwise a little by 'snapping' the wrists (left rotating to the inside, right extending forward in this case). This kind of compound rotation through multiple planes at the same time will often produce unfamiliar cracking noises as tendons experience previously undiscovered ranges of motion!

SMALL CIRCLE EXERCISE—WRIST EXTENSIONS II

Like many foundation pieces, the wrist extension exercises contain multiple lessons. In addition to teaching **two-way action** when practiced at normal speed, accelerating them—as Professor Leon routinely does at the end of each set—is great **wrist snap** practice, and pulling back slightly at the end of the inside and outside versions helps to perfect hooking ...

○ **Small Circle Practice Pointer:** Grip up with a twisting motion to tighten the grasp—then snap the wrists sharply in the appropriate direction just prior to executing the technique. Motion starts in the little finger and the knuckles dig into the opponent's body.

VIII. PULSING AND WAVING:
Redirection of Force

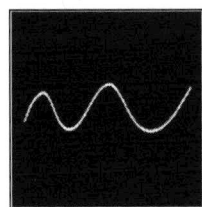

From time-to-time, every martial arts practitioner encounters a student who seems impervious to a given technique or group of techniques. Sometimes it is the double-jointed individual whose limbs can be bent to alarming angles without seeming to cause the slightest discomfort. At other times it may be a person who can be repeatedly struck directly on a pressure point without producing any observable effect. Frustrating as this can be, it presents an opportunity to delve into some of the more arcane teachings of the art of Small Circle Jujitsu, among which are **'pulsing' and 'waving'**.

As discussed in greater detail in the first appendix to this work, human beings have a variety of ways of experiencing and managing pain. When a pain-compliance technique does not seem to work at first, it may be that the stimulus has not yet reached the opponent's pain threshold (minimum level) or has not exceeded his pain tolerance (maximum level). Both of these problems can be addressed by **pulsing** and **waving**.

○ **Small Circle Practice Pointer:**

Pulsing involves varying the level of pressure or energy applied.

Waving involves varying the type or direction of pressure or energy.

Using the basic wrist lock, for example, if the desired pain response is not immediately produced, the advanced Small Circle practitioner knows how to decrease and then rapidly increase the torque being applied *using a broken rhythm* (**pulsing**) and vary the angle of application of that torque (**waving**).

Pressure point resistance presents a somewhat more complex problem, for which **pulsing and waving** may nevertheless present a valid solution. There is a small percentage of the population on whom pressure points seem to have a diminished effect or none at all, at least when those points are activated with a conventional application of force. Advanced pressure point fighters, however, learn to control the energy with which they strike, effectively **pulsing** and **waving** in this context as well. Those who can achieve this level of energetic control experience far more success working with naturally resistant people, and exponentially increase the effectiveness of their techniques when engaging with normally reactive opponents (who make up a far greater percentage of the population).

SMALL CIRCLE EXERCISE—RESISTING IN TWO DIRECTIONS

A simple way to demonstrate (and practice) this principle is to have the opponent grab and attempt to immobilize your wrist. Even with two hands. No matter how strong the opponent, if you apply pressure in one direction and then suddenly reverse course, or rapidly modulate the intensity of the pressure being applied, you will almost always break through the resistance.

IX. THE CASCADE EFFECT:
Acceleration of Pain

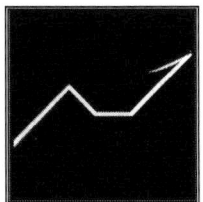

A **cascade** is a series of occurrences, each of which builds upon the preceding one. A simple example of this principle in play is experienced by anyone who suffers the agony that the lightest touch can produce when the body is already tender from a pre-existing condition like a torn ligament, a damaged tooth, or even a simple stubbed toe. The pain of the existing condition may have subsided to near imperceptibility, and a light tap would normally produce nothing more than a momentary distraction, but when the two come together, the effect can be incapacitating. And when the number of stimuli in the **cascade** increases to three, four, or five, the effects range from debilitating to deadly...

A cascade effect is an inevitable, and sometimes unforeseen, chain of events that results from an action affecting a system. The [negative] impact of the cascade effect on a system can be analyzed using consequence/impact analysis:

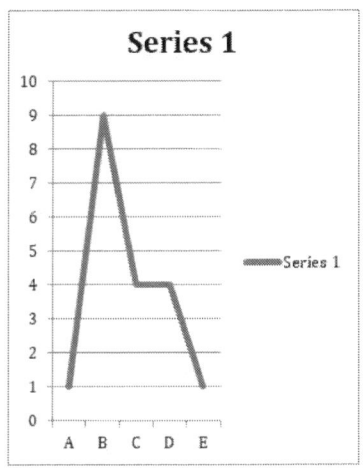

Point A	Nerve at rest
Point A-B	Stimulus applied
Point B	Maximum pain response to stimulus
Point B-C	Recovery
Point C-D	Recovery plateau as nerve repolarizes
Point D-E	Full repolarization
Point E	Nerve at rest

Diagram 1 shows a normal nerve reaction to a particular stimulus. Pain is carried to the brain by the spinal cord.[1] The stimulus causes peak pain response (B) before falling away (from B to C), plateauing briefly (from C-D), and then returning to its original level (E).[2]

[1.] Via the spino-thalamic tract in the case of light stimulus and the dorsal columns in the case of deep pain.

[2.] It should be noted that a nerve must reset ("repolarize") this way before it is able to carry any additional stimuli. This essentially involves charged elemental atoms—primarily calcium—crossing back out of the nerve.

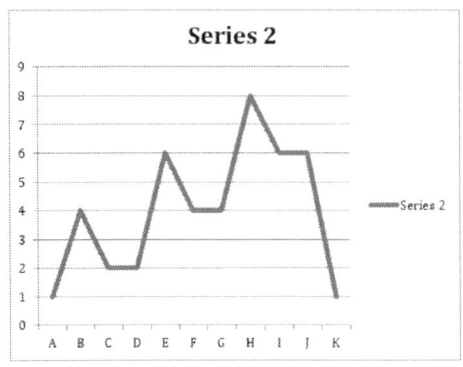

Series 2

A	Nerve at rest
A-B	Stimulus applied
B	Maximum pain response
C-D	Plateau
D	New stimulus applied
D-E	Increased pain response
F-G	Plateau
G	Further stimulus applied
H	Marked increase in pain response
I-J	Plateau
J-K	Repolarization
K	Nerve at rest

Diagram 2, by contrast, shows that if additional stimuli are applied at the end of the plateau phases (C to D; F to G…), a much higher pain peak-stimulus can be achieved.

In common experience, we know that if we have a toothache, and the tongue happens to touch the sore spot, the pain is amplified exponentially. This same effect is utilized in Small Circle Jujitsu in many and various ways. As an initial matter, we learn repetition sequences, which are stored in the cerebellum, one move leading inevitably to another. But the most powerful application of this effect can be seen in the production of pain; a principle that the Professors Jay use to their advantage. For example, rubbing a nerve point with the knuckles back-and-forth, fracturing an already dislocated joint, or repeatedly applying a finger lock—all of these are practical examples of the cascade effect in action.

—Dr. Phil Courtney, 7th Dan

DIFFERENT DISCIPLINES

Cascade theory applies in a wide range of contexts, from international economics to the functioning of natural phenomena to the practice of medicine. There is an exponential, logarithmic compounding effect when we add 'insult' to an initial 'injury'. With very little additional input, the adverse effect on the recipient is extremely, and often dramatically, disproportionate. Even if we apply successively less force or impact, the first contact at a strategic point may be painful, the second much more so, the third may be devastating, and the fourth may be deadly. We have seen this repeatedly in our observations and experiences. This is true both subjectively and objectively. Like the aerodynamics of the Bumble bee, this phenomenon may seem to defy the laws of physics, but it works far more often that it fails. It is more than cumulative. It is a crescendo with a desired totally disproportionate climax effect.

○ **In Nature:** A waterfall which operates in stages where each 'fall' feeds the next until they eventually all combine.

○ **In Economics:** A phenomenon in which a particular good is taxed at each stage of production, thereby increasing the tax-value at each successive stage.

○ **In Physiology:** A sequence of successive activation reactions involving enzymes (enzyme cascade) or hormones (hormone cascade) characterized by a series of amplifications of an initial stimulus. In blood coagulation, for example, each enzyme activates the next until the final product, the fibrin clot, is reached.

○ **In Engineering:** A cascade amplifier is a series of stages in the processing chain of an electrical signal where each operates the next in turn (as a modifier). This cumulative process is responsible for the formation of an electrical discharge, cosmic-ray shower, or Geiger counter avalanche.

○ **In Psychology:** A situation in which one complaint (illness for example) aggravates another (depression) which, in turn, aggravates another (employability) in a malicious cycle.

—Dr. Harvey Levy, 2nd Dan

Professor Wally touched on this concept in his first book, where he wrote: "*Energy transfer breaks your opponent's resistance more effectively than if you were to apply force to the area of focus immediately... An example of energy transfer is the application of the reverse arm-bar, using knuckles against your opponent's triceps tendon. First, use a heavy palm by pressing your palm heavily against the opponent's forearm below his elbow. Then transfer the energy from there to the point of focus above the elbow, driving your knuckles directly into the tendon of the triceps.*"

—Professor Wally Jay, <u>Small Circle Jujitsu</u> (O'Hara, 1989).

o **Small Circle Practice Pointer:** Orchestrate your attack so that a combination of techniques build together to trigger the cascade effect. For example: In applying a simple arm bar, torque the points around the wrist 'manacle' (LU-8, PE-6, HT-6, TW-6-7-8) with the gripping hand before pulling, and position the forearm fulcrum by striking above the elbow (TW-12) before sliding down to the joint (TW-11) to push/lever.

X. WHIPLASH STRIKING:
The Push-Pull Principle

It is not uncommon in the realm of Eastern philosophy to find answers in opposites (as in: *"If you wish to hold onto something, you must let it go"*; or *"When you enter, think of leaving"*). The same is often true of performing certain techniques, at least at more advanced levels. In the realm of striking, perhaps the dictum should be: *"When you wish to push forward, think of pulling back."*

Anyone who has received a strike from either of the Professors Jay during training knows that while these gentlemen are best known for their throwing and locking abilities, their punches and kicks can also be devastating. When delivered in earnest, it feels as though the hand or foot has actually penetrated the body and made direct contact with the nerves within! This is the result of the application of a variety of energetic techniques, one of which is the 'push-pull' principle or so-called "**whiplash**" method of striking.

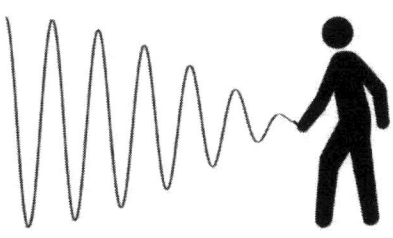

Western scientific methods have demonstrated that in the hands of a capable person, the handle of a bullwhip being manipulated at speeds of no more than a hundred miles per hour can cause the loop to exceed *two times the speed of sound (over 1,500 mph)!* This is so, at least in part, because of the 'push-pull' method which is used to make the whip crack. The **"whiplash strike"** achieves a similar type of amplification, in a similar way. By 'pushing' the body-weapon forward with a loose and fluid movement, and then 'snapping' it back sharply at the point of impact, the penetrating force of the strike can be increased exponentially (similar to the Chinese concept of *'fa jing'*).

> ○ **Small Circle Practice Pointer:** Strike with a loose hand, tightening up and retracting slightly at the point of impact.

SMALL CIRCLE EXERCISE—CANDLE PRACTICE

With sufficient practice, it is possible to extinguish the flame of a candle by striking toward it without ever making physical contact. This can be done with any number of strikes. The key, however, is not the forward motion of the technique, but the *insertion* and the *retraction*. Using a simple punch as an example, the feeling should not be to 'blow' the flame out with the forward pressure of the fist, but rather to 'suck' it out with a snapping withdrawal.

Just as flicking water off the fingertips is not the same thing as energy projection, but helps to give students a sense of the feeling they are working toward, so extinguishing the candle's flame in this manner is not, in and of itself, whiplash striking, but it is a pretty good first step toward that goal…

XI. ENTRIES AND EXITS:
Bookending the Technique

In watching Professor Leon—and before him, Professor Wally—performing techniques on the mat, it becomes clear over time that a skillful set-up (entry) and a powerful follow-up (exit) are almost as important to victory as is the technique itself.

Entries (the Set-up): The power of this principle is perhaps most easily recognized in the context of throws, where a sufficiently deep and powerful entry (*tsukuri*) can off-balance the opponent to such a degree that the final "push" of execution (*kake*) is almost an afterthought. But throws are not the only type of techniques where a proper set-up is helpful.

○ In locking, the manipulation of the limb prior to the application of the technique can make a significant difference to the ultimate effect (as with **energy transfer**).

○ In neck restraints, the effect of any previous impact on the opponent's respiratory and circulatory systems makes a significant difference in the efficacy of the technique (as with keeping the opponent off balance/winded).

○ And in striking, employing a particular pattern can make the resulting reaction far exceed the sum of its parts (as with the **cascade effect**).

○ For a detailed examination of practical entry methodology, *see* John Mellon's contribution to Chapter XX of this work.

SMALL CIRCLE EXERCISE—TSUKURI

A good tool for testing and improving **entries** is the practice of pausing after the set-up and before the execution to see how little additional force or energy is required to achieve the desired result. For example, when performing *O Soto Gari*, a sufficiently brisk and deep entry will almost topple the opponent all by itself, even before the application of any upper-body technique.

THE CHECK HAND

A vital part of every entry is making sure to avoid walking into an attack (first: do no harm). Notice how the master practitioners often employ a checking hand to forestall the opponent's attack/counter-attack when making entry ...

> o **Small Circle Practice Pointer:** Keeping the opponent off balance as much as possible while remaining on balance yourself will drain his energy reserves quickly while preserving your own. This, in turn, will make the subsequent application of any given technique that much easier and more effective.

Exits (the Follow-up): Just as important as how Small Circle practitioners set up their techniques is how they follow them up or finish them off. Again, watching Professor Wally and Professor Leon's own performance is highly instructive in this regard. Never do they simply end the technique as if presenting it in a vacuum. There is always some form of follow-on technique, even if it is just a defensive withdrawal from the field of engagement.

A wise sword master once said: *"When in doubt, cut down. If still in doubt, cut down again!"* Among the several lessons this ancient dictum imparts is the idea that doing *something*—even something simple—is almost always preferable to doing nothing. The practitioner does not need to have a vast array of techniques to call upon in order to perform an effective follow-up. Something as simple as a final fist-strike or a defensive step-back will qualify. What is essential is that the Small Circle student does not simply drop his guard and turn his back on the threat...

> o **Classical Jujitsu Practice Pointer:** "After the battle, tighten your helmet cords!"

XII. HEALING:
The House of Pain

There is a long and venerable tradition in the martial arts of pairing the science of harming with the practice of healing. Not only is there a certain symmetry to being able to undo any injury that has been inflicted; there is also often significant overlap in the techniques employed. It should come as no surprise, then, that Henry Okazaki—Professor Wally's Danzan Ryu Jujitsu teacher—was also a master of a healing system known as "Seifukujutsu."

Professor Wally and his wife Bernice (herself a 9th Degree Black Belt) learned and attained mastery in both the martial and the healing arts taught by Okazaki Sensei.

Before even meeting Professor Wally, however, Bernice had learned *"lomi-lomi"* massage, and other forms of traditional Hawaiian medicine, from her Great Aunt Maile Moku; an experienced healer in the community. Her initial interest in the martial arts was piqued at the age of fourteen when a judo instructor offered to teach this art to her and a group of her friends, but coming from a very traditional family, such a young girl was not permitted to engage in this kind of training with a *male* teacher.

Years later, after meeting Professor Wally, Bernice began training with him and his teachers, in her words, "so that I would know what they were talking about!" For years she studied the arts of harming and healing alongside her husband, attaining senior ranking in both Danzan Ryu Jujitsu and the accompanying healing art of Seifukujutsu. She and Professor Wally even attended special black belt classes together at which it was forbidden to take any notes!

Bernice's powerful deep tissue massage, combined with the usual training bumps and bruises that required such treatment, caused the Jay dojo to become known as, "The House of Pain!" "The healing arts," she notes, "went hand in hand with the martial arts" in both the Okazaki dojo and the Jay household. Over the years she successfully treated many of the Professor's friends and students, including a mechanic who was unable to return to work after an arm injury, and a young boy with polio who lived on Professor Wally's mail route.

The Seifukujutsu method is a type of restorative massage that aims to break down and rebuild muscle tissue over time, while also stimulating the body's energy channels. The energetic aspects of the art are similar to acupuncture or shiatsu. The deep tissue massage is performed using a rocking, ironing, or pulsing movement with the forearm or elbow, and also employs many other parts of the body, including the hands and even feet in the form of back-walking. It is greatly assisted by the application of a special liniment formulated by Master Okazaki known as *"satsuzai"* (or more colloquially, "bug juice").

> ○ **Small Circle Practice Pointer:** The "heat" of *satsuzai* can be dialed up by increasing the amount of wintergreen, or decreased by adding more olive oil, which will also increase the "slipperiness" of the formula...

Bernice recalls that Professor Wally was always coming up with new ideas and innovative solutions to martial challenges. Sometimes he would wake up in the middle of the night, having discovered a piece of the puzzle in a dream-state, and begin frantically jotting down notes before the image faded. "For him," she says, "it was always about helping his students to become the best they could be." When asked if she ever grew weary of her husband's constant training, she simply says, "No..."

> ○ **Small Circle Practice Pointer:** Pure mustard can be used as a remedy for aches and bruises. The plaster should be left on until the heat becomes almost unbearable!

BODY WORK

My appreciation of massage therapy came primarily from Bernice Jay (Wally's wife)—she was amazing—she could launch you to a different physical level, pushing you right up to the edge of the pain threshold! To this day, I still look for 'body-workers' of the same caliber…

—Guro Dan Inosanto

XIII. ADDITIONAL PRECEPTS:
The Art Within the Art

In the practice of Small Circle Jujitsu, it would be hard to conceive of better guidelines than the Principles laid out by the Professors Jay. This is not to say, however, that these are the *only* concepts that students of this way should study. Variations, and indeed innovations, comprise important aspects of the well-rounded practitioner's portfolio. If they are not sufficiently distinct to qualify as 'principles' in their own right, then perhaps they can be considered 'precepts'…

I. <u>Ever-decreasing/Accelerating Spiral [Rotational Momentum]</u>:

○ While the name of the art is Small *Circle* Jujitsu, in practice, the effect of applying a small circle is vastly improved if it is a circle with an ever-decreasing circumference: a small *spiral*, particularly when the both cause and effect contribute to *accelerating* that spiral as it is applied.

II.   *Kuzushi* [Breaking Balance]:

o **Triangle Theory:** As previously discussed, no matter what stance a person adopts, there can be only two points of contact with the ground. As a result, there will always be a third point—in fact two such points— that are perpendicular to the balance line between the feet. Learning to 'see' these tipping points helps the Small Circle practitioner determine where the opponent's balance can be most easily broken.

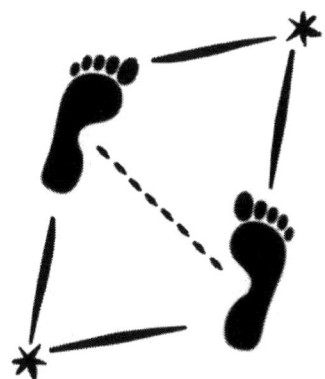

o **Eight Directional Theory:** While the *easiest* path to breaking the opponent's balance is usually along the line that is perpendicular to the balance points, *any* stance can be unbalanced in all eight directions with sufficient effort (North, South, West, East, NE, NW, SE, SW).

○ **Twenty-four Directional Theory:** This also works in three dimensions (West-Up, West-Middle, West-Down, East-Up, East-Middle, East-Down…).

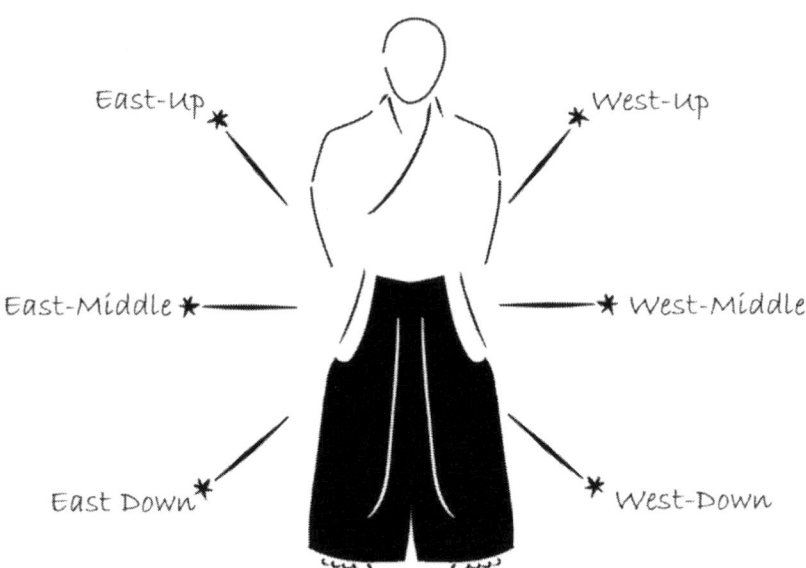

III. Making Space & Taking Space (Forward Pressure) [Mobility]:

○ **Taking Space:** Controlling the space between combatants is an essential tool of the well-trained martial artist. When applying a technique, the attacker needs to ensure that there are no openings within which the defender can mount a counter-offensive. Watching the way Professor Leon molds his body to his opponent when applying a neck restraint, for example, is instructive in this regard.

More broadly, this precept may be thought of as: "Maintaining forward pressure whenever possible and advantageous to do so…"

○ **Making Space:** Conversely, when resisting an attack, the defender must *create* space, not only to avoid being hit, but also to be able to maneuver in order to counter and escape.

○ **Small Circle Practice Pointer:** When performing *tsukuri*, mold yourself to your opponent like a constrictor encircling its prey.

○ *Making* Space **In Order to** *Take* **Space**: Particularly in the realm of throwing, it is often necessary to create enough space to allow *nag*e to push or pull *uke* off balance. If the opponent's balance is not broken by the time of the entry, entering too closely leaves no room in which to perform the essential process of *kuzushi*.

Uke: The partner who receives the technique (often the student).

Tori/Nage: The partner who performs the technique/throw.

IV. Complex Levers (Complex Torque) [Fulcrum, Lever & Base]:

○ **Compound Lever**: This is an incredibly powerful technique for enhancing leverage exponentially by using the motion achieved by the first lever to act as the 'effort' for the second. Nail-clippers operate using this principle. In the martial realm, using a finger lock to move the hand in such a way as to apply the pressure required for a larger wrist or arm lock has roughly the same effect.

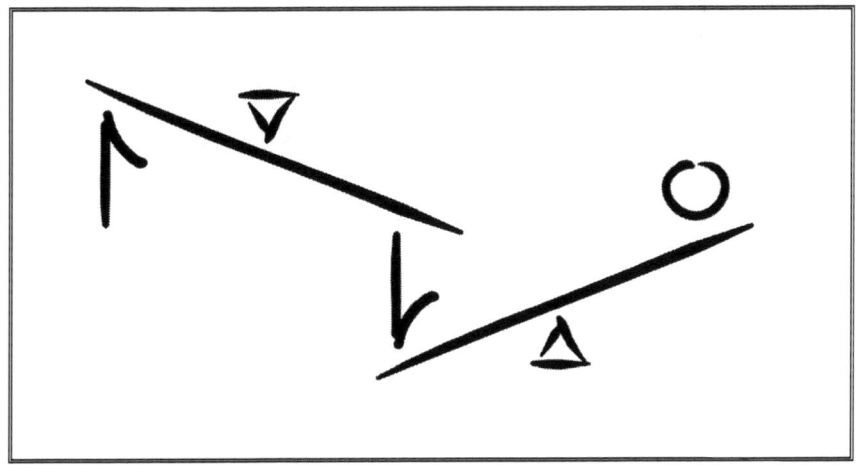

○ **Double Lever:** This mechanism applies leverage in two separate places on the limb at the same time rather than having one power the other. A good example would be augmenting a bent-elbow wrist lock with a wrist compression. While one lock does not necessarily facilitate the other, their combined effect is *significantly* greater.

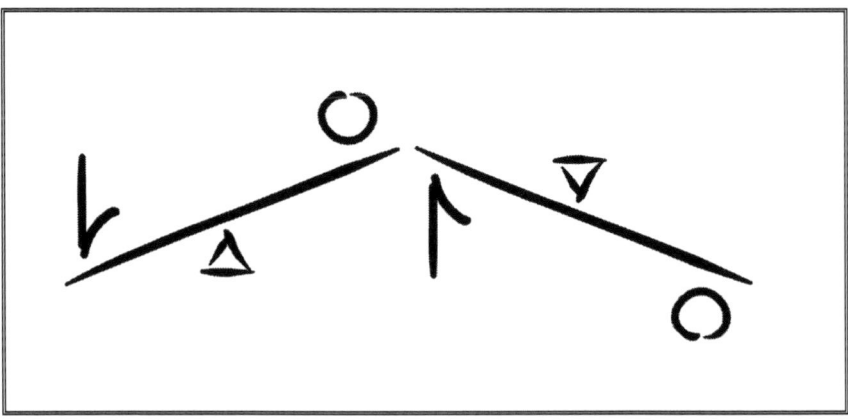

V. Combat Stance/Guard:

○ In many martial arts systems, the formal stances, guard positions, and blocking techniques—while helpful as training tools for various purposes—are far from realistic representations of effective fighting methods. Imagine, for example, entering the octagon and immediately sinking into a deep and static *kiba dachi* while your opponent bounces around you, and then trying to block his flurry of jabs with a semi-circular *uchi-uke* that tracks a path from your opposite hip all the way to just in front of your lead shoulder...

Not surprisingly, Small Circle practitioners are taught to apply a much more agile and fluid combat methodology:

• The fighting stance is relatively high and shallow (balls of the feet for mobility) and maintains forward pressure to support hand attacks;

• The hands form a guard shaped a little like drawbridge closing at the centerline, with the elbows near the 'wood-ocean' and palms cupped and facing outward to maximize speed, control, and sensitivity.

• The block for most attacks is then executed by simply snapping one of the open palms in/down to check (at launch-point), parry (at mid-point), or slip (at end-point)…

VI. Check the Threat:

○ All too often, inexperienced martial artists focus too sharply on the move they are attempting to perform, but fail to account for the opponent's efforts to frustrate that performance. Professor Leon, however, invariably takes the additional step of checking any hand (or other limb) that might conceivably counter his technique.

VII. Gravity Wells:

○ Another product of that most under-rated of training methods—*mitorigeiko*—is an appreciation for the way in which true masters can supercharge their techniques by allowing gravity to do much of the work for them. Watch, for example, how Professor Leon drops his entire body weight into the execution of certain locking techniques (like the inverted finger lock).

VIII. Cutting the Central Axis:

○ Imagine a vertical line that more-or-less tracks the spine—this is the body's central axis. By angling techniques to intersect ("cut") this line, the practitioner can ensure proper angle and direction for application of almost any technique.

XIV. PRESSURE POINTS:
The Target

During the 1980's—a decade characterized in many ways by selfishness—a truly remarkable alliance emerged on the North American martial arts scene. Professor Wally Jay combined forces with headmasters of several other systems in order to share skills, seminars, and students. For many years, these senior masters traveled the country, and indeed the world, in various combinations, spreading their teachings, and a generation of martial artists is richer for it. Among the members of this council of masters were Remy Presas (Modern Arnis/Filipino Stick Fighting), George Dillman (Ryukyu Kempo/Pressure Point Fighting), and Leo Fong (Wei Kuen Do/Kung Fu).

And while each system already contained elements of the others, it is undeniable that a kind of martial cross-pollination took place over the years and decades that followed, enriching each art along the way. For example, even though Professor Wally had already learned the power of striking certain special targets (such as what Okazaki Sensei taught as: "Third Sensitive"), the breadth and depth of the pressure point material in the current SCJ syllabus owes a great deal to this early association.

·◇· WILL HIGGINBOTHAM ·◇·

THE PRESSURE POINT CONNECTION

When Professor Wally Jay first met karate master George Dillman, it only took a short time for him to realize that what Dillman was teaching about pressure points could enhance his newly created baby, Small Circle Jujitsu. He saw that using the concepts of pressure points greatly improved the success of almost all of his grappling techniques by taking advantage of the inherent weaknesses of the human body. Professor Jay was already using many of these point locations from years of trial-and-error training to find the best ways to perform a given technique, but he didn't know about the acupressure point locations and how reliable it was to find them. At Professor Jay's seminars, and at any of the "Big Three" camps, Professor Jay would talk to the senior Dillman students from time-to-time to further his knowledge of pressure points. He also tasked his son, Leon, with learning this method so that he could help him incorporate this information into the family system.

The Basics: Three things are important in beginning to understand pressure point principles and practices.

1. Physical *location of the point*;
2. The *type of pressure* needed to activate a given point;
3. The *angle and direction* needed to apply the pressure.

There are three types of pressure that activate pressure points.

1. **Touch**: A steady push or pressure;
2. **Rub**: A stroking motion or a vibration;
3. **Strike**: A sudden tap or percussion.

There are **twelve meridians** and **eight vessels**. A meridian is a channel or pathway of energy that flows through the body. A vessel is a channel that stores energy. Only two of the eight vessels are present on the surface of the body: the Conception and the Governor vessel. The twelve meridians are bilateral; they exist on both sides of the body. Professor Dillman teaches that there are 361 places on the body that can be activated for self-defense.

There are also two more sets of points that were discovered long after the original points. These are **"the miscellaneous points"** and **"the new points."** These two categories of points are mostly found along the original meridians, but the original meridians were not renumbered. Instead, these points were given their own numbers combined with the part of the body where they are located. So, M-HN-18 means Miscellaneous Point-Head and Neck-number 18. With these extra points figured in, the total number of points available for use climbs to more than double the original points.

The concepts found in the study of Five Element Acupuncture are used to make the pressure points work even better in grappling, throwing or striking. We use the **Cycle of Destruction**, the **Cycle of Creation**, **Yin & Yang Theory**, and **Diurnal Cycle** principles in the execution of Small Circle Jujitsu techniques.

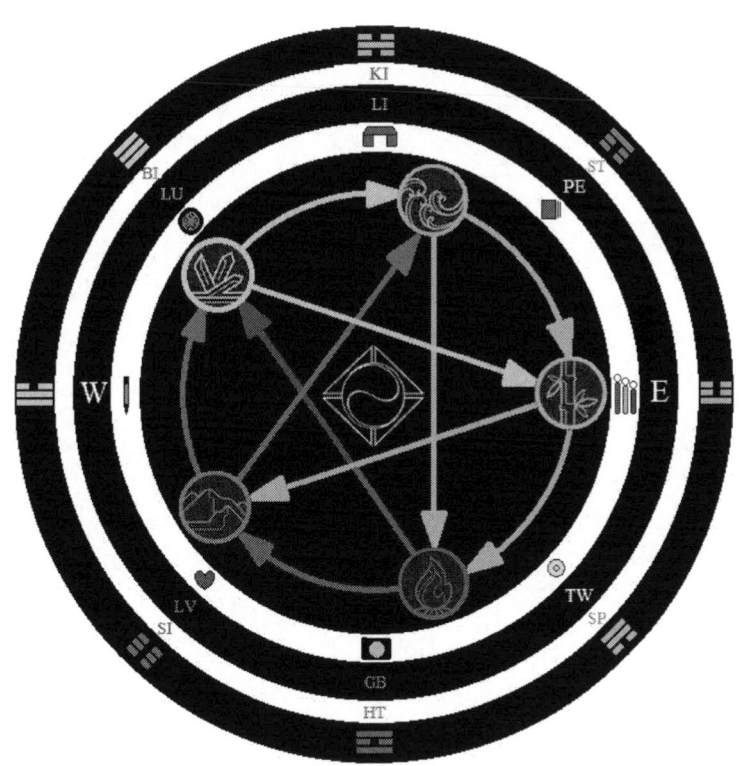

In this text we are only talking about the usage and total buy-in of Small Circle Jujitsu concerning the use of pressure points. A more complete study of pressure points pertaining to martial arts can be found in any book by Professor George Dillman and Chris Thomas. They are the best books available anywhere to further your study and understanding of pressure point usage.

Grappling: There are a few ways that the use of pressure points can enhance the execution of techniques. Generally, the use of pressure points can make the attacker weaker or more pliable to enable the defender to perform a controlling technique.

> **Example—hammer lock from a straight punch:** The punch is with the attacker's right fist. We would slap down on his right forearm with our left palm activating the points of the "Triple Warmer V" (TW-5, 6, 7 & 8). At the same time, we slap the upper arm on Large Intestine points (LI-11, 12 & 13 plus a few new and miscellaneous points). This opening action weakens the whole arm in two ways:
>
> 1. Attacking the Triple Warmer meridian weakens the whole arm (and we're hitting four points there).
>
> 2. Triple Warmer is the element "Fire". The Large Intestine points are "Metal". In the Cycle of Destruction rule, "Fire Melts Metal" also causing weakness in that arm. So, after the first hit, the arm is weakened to allow us to manipulate it.
>
> Next, we grab Heart Two with our right fingers and pull the attacker forward, turning him for the lock. This happens while snaking the left hand around the forearm and following through with the blade of the left hand slicing over Heart Three in the elbow joint. The subsequent move to secure the lock is to brush up the upper arm of the attacker with your right hand (sending Lung energy backward towards Lung One and Two) then quickly cutting into Lung One and Two to prevent the attacker from bending over while cinching up the lock.
>
> In this example, the points were used to make the technique work against the attacker's will. The opening move destroyed the energy of the arm. Pulling on Heart Two made his whole body shift the way you wanted him to move using pain compliance it *really* hurts to press on HT-2)! The final security of the technique is to stroke the right hand up the arm and cut into Lung One and Two to prevent the attacker from bending forward to escape the pain of the lock.

> To explain every technique in this detail would fill a very large volume. Instead, the student of this arts needs to train with an instructor that is capable of teaching the correct principles needed to be effective in executing these techniques.

Striking: Professor Wally Jay always said that you can do anything in Small Circle Jujitsu. That means you can grapple, strike or throw. The old expression, "Hit to lock or lock to hit" comes into play here. Striking pressure points during an attack opens opportunities for either grappling, throwing (including take downs), or striking for different follow ups. In the example above, striking was used to enable an opportunity to grapple, but striking can be the beginning and end result as well. In this case we can "attack the attack and then attack the attacker".

> **Example—two-arm shove to the chest:** Assuming you noticed some sort of pre-assault cue, you would have at least one arm bent upward to protect your head. Upon seeing the attacker's arms coming forward, you would divide them while striking each arm. Using open hands, you would strike down on the Large Intestine points of one arm while striking upwards on the Lung points of the other arm.
>
> The next move is to slap down on Stomach Five with the high hand, and up on Stomach Five with the low hand. This action follows the Diurnal Cycle by striking Lung, Large Intestine, and then unloading on Stomach. Striking both sides of the body incorporates the Yin & Yang principle as well. Performed properly, this technique can cause dizziness, disorientation, or even unconsciousness.

Throwing: As with grappling, anytime a throw is executed, pressure points can be used for control, distraction, and weakening. Disorienting an opponent will buy precious seconds to give a big advantage to the defender.

> **Example—hip throw (*o goshi*) from a punch attack:** When an attack is launched, we often use a "shutdown" to stop the attack and then throw the attacker to the ground (or the shutdown may not be needed when taking advantage of an attacker's forward momentum). While executing *o goshi* from a punch, the defender tries to get his hip into position by reaching *behind* the attacker and pulling on the bottom floating rib (GB-25). The pain from this action forces the attacker to shift his body over for the hip throw.

Even the "referee position" has advantages when using pressure points. While holding the opponent's sleeve, you can place your knuckles on the Large Intestine points of the upper arm. When you feel the opponent try move you, you react by pushing on LI-11 or LI-12 which pins his elbow to his body and controls him. Using the other hand that is placed on the opponent's collar, you can roll your grip inward to press on his ST-9 & 10.

Professor Leon Jay incorporates pressure points and manipulation using *qi* (*chi*) control wherever needed. If you have an innate knowledge of the body and its weaknesses, you will use that information to empower you to be more effective. Small Circle Jujitsu is not a sport. It is a very practical approach to protecting yourself using principles laid down by Professor Wally Jay, now being carried forward by Professor Leon Jay. I know his father would be proud of how his son has spread his art around the world…

—Will Higginbotham, 7th Dan

To this day, Professor Leon continues to require students to demonstrate the ability to employ pressure point striking techniques as part of the Small Circle curriculum. Simply memorizing the location of a point, however, is not nearly enough. As students progress through the ranks, they are expected to learn the proper method of activation, the anticipated effect of stimulation, and the characteristics of the point in the system as a whole. A few examples are provided below.

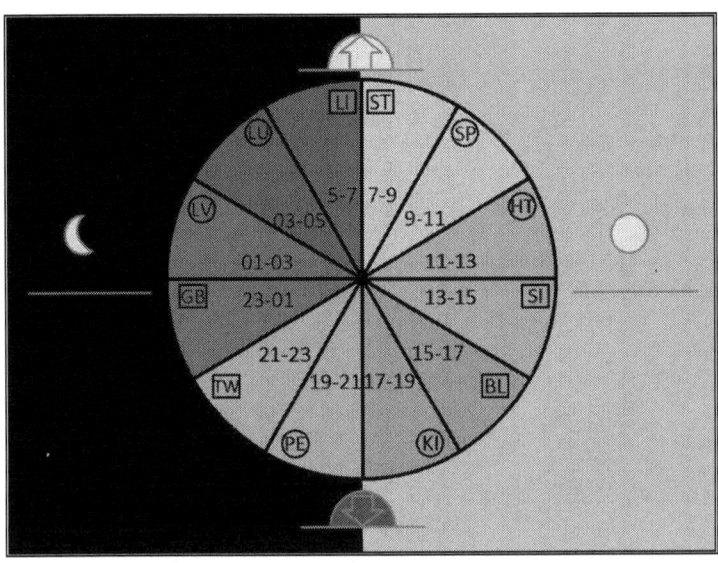

Name	Location	Method	Effect	Characteristics
Heart -2	Inside arm above elbow	Strike ↓	Bends arm	Fire, yin, midday
Heart-6	Inside wrist pinky side	Touch ↓	Bends wrist	Fire, yin, midday
Lung-5	Inside forearm below elbow	Strike ✓	Buckle knee	Metal, yin, 3-5 am
Lung-8	Inside wrist thumb side	Press ↓	Bends wrist	Metal, yin, 3-5 am
TW-11	Outside arm above elbow	Rub ↓	Bends body	Fire, yang, 9-11 pm
TW-12	Middle of triceps	Strike ↓	Bends body	Fire, yang, 9-11 pm
BL-10	Lateral border trapezius	Strike ✓	Knocks out	Water, yang, 3-5 pm
BL-57	Middle of calf muscle	Press ↓	Pins leg	Water, yang, 3-5 pm

THE EYE OF THE BEHOLDER

Whether these principles actually explain the true nature of reality or merely describe the effects of some more concrete force at work, the fact remains that they provide an invaluable analytical tool to the practitioner. In order to be promoted to *shodan* and beyond in Small Circle Jujitsu, for example, students are required to unlock the secrets of pressure point fighting, and it is these ancient theories that provide them with the key.

XV. WEAPONS:
Sticks and Other Weapons

Both Professor Wally and Professor Leon were close friends of Professor Remy Presas—the founder of the Filipino art of Modern Arnis—and both Headmasters in their time embraced this remarkable man and his art, weaving it into the syllabus of Small Circle Jujitsu.

While Modern Arnis is a total system, teaching empty hand techniques alongside weapons training, it is perhaps best known for its employment of the rattan cane. The impact of the stick-fighting component of his art on the Small Circle syllabus is clear, manifesting itself in requirements of increasing difficulty as the student progresses through the ranks. By the time Small Circle practitioners earn their black belts, they have learned Modern Arnis's twelve basic strikes and the corresponding counters and disarms; the circular cyclical striking pattern of *redonda;* and the sinuous weaving style of the *sinawali* method.

It is no accident that cane-fighting techniques form such an essential part of the curricula of both Modern Arnis and Small Circle Jujitsu. The reason behind this shared characteristic is that both arts prepare practitioners to confront real-world threats, where blades and sticks are commonly-encountered weapons.

MODERN ARNIS

In 2019, at the annual U.S. East Coast Camp, Professor Leon officially designated **Master of Tapi-Tapi Ken Smith** as the Technical Director of the Modern Arnis component of Small Circle Jujitsu. In so doing, he cemented for all time the importance of this art within his family system.

While Modern Arnis is a complete, standalone system in its own right (*see* Modern Arnis: History & Practice), many of its weapons-based basic forms lend themselves perfectly to supplementing primarily empty-hand styles. In his capacity as Technical Director, Master Smith has recently identified several such forms that should be studied by Small Circle students:

THE TWELVE STRIKING ANGLES

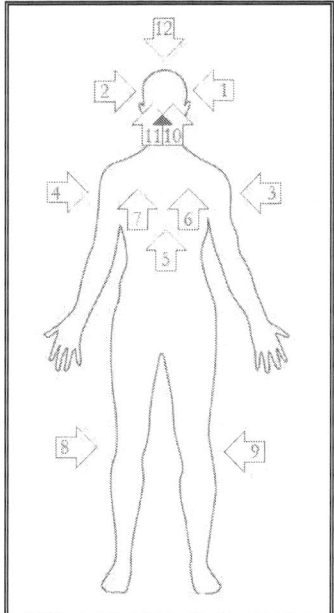

BLOCK-CHECK-COUNTER

○ One of the fundamental weapons defenses, **Block-Check-Counter** teaches that when A attacks, B blocks with his own weapon; B's 'live' hand checks the opponent's weapon hand; and B's weapon hand counters.

SINAWALI (SINGLE)

○ One of the fundamental striking forms, *Sinawali* (weaving) teaches alternating high-against-high/low-against-low striking/defending in a continuous pattern.

REDONDA (DOUBLE)

○ One of the fundamental striking forms, *Redonda* (rounding) teaches striking/defending in a flowing pattern of three circular strikes. It can be practiced individually (single) against fixed targets or in tandem (double) against moving targets.

DISARMS (NUMBER ONE)

○ One of the fundamental weapon defenses, **Disarms** deprive the opponent of his weapon. Disarm #1: Weapon blocks weapon; 'live' hand traps opponent's weapon; with a pull/twist/push motion, the opponent's weapon is stripped away. Together with disarms #2, #5 and #12, these techniques will serve to defend against most attacks.

TRAPPING HANDS

○ One of the fundamental empty-hand forms, **Trapping Hands** improves speed, sensitivity, and timing: Here, the near hand blocks the strike; the far hand checks; the near hand counters; and so on...

SLAP-OFF/PULL-OFF

○ In **Slap-off/Pull-off**, when the opponent blocks the initial strike, the attacker pulls or slaps the block away hand away (depending on angle; here, pulls) so as to clear a path for the attack to continue to its intended target.

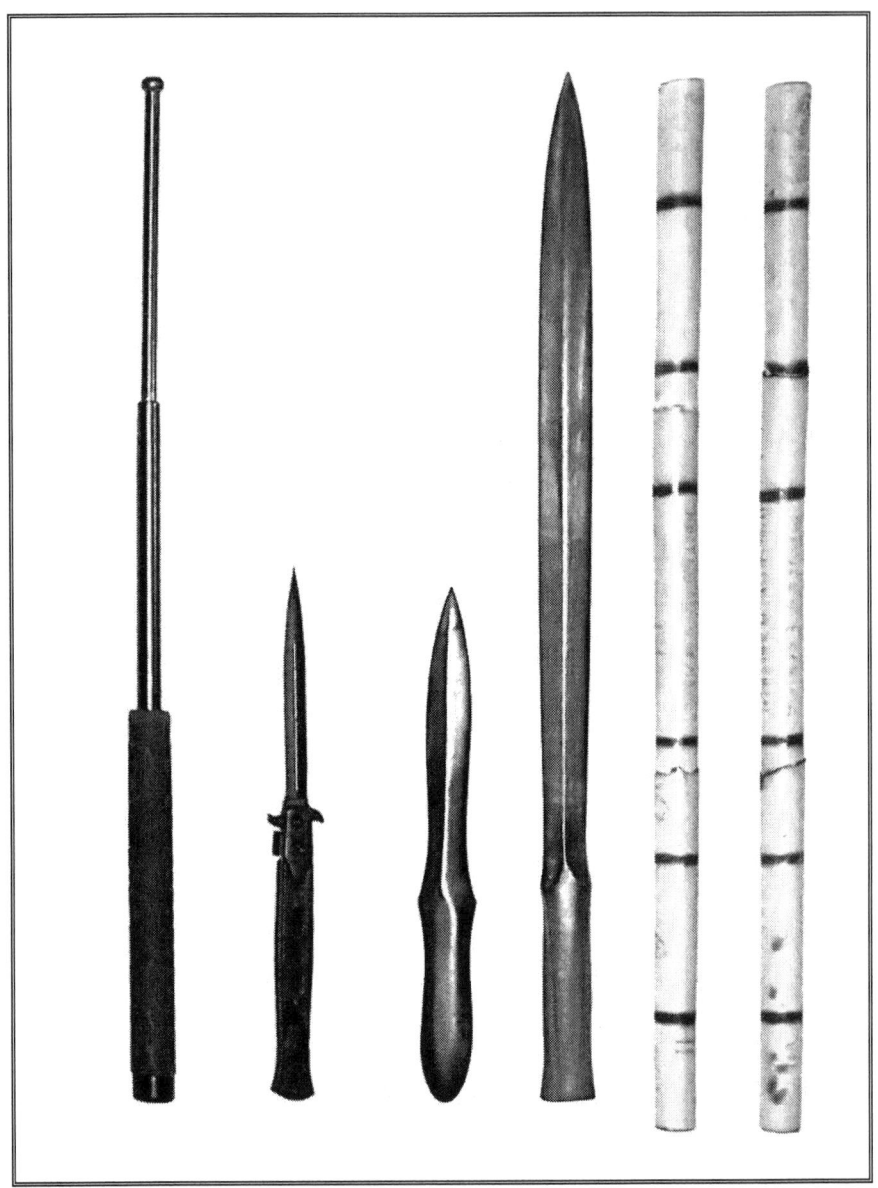

WHAT WOULD YOU CHANGE?

Professor Leon once said that if he could change any aspect of his martial journey, he would have spent more time training with Remy Presas. In this regard, it is interesting to note that one of the most fundamental elements of Remy Presas' art was "finding the [**transitional**] **flow**…"

◆ DAVE CASTOLDI ◆

WEAPONS

I met Professor Jay for the first time in 1977. My instructor at the time—John Wooten at the Hoko Judo club—told me that this sixty-five year old master would be coming in to teach a clinic, and I remember thinking to myself at the time, "What is *he* going to teach *me*?" I was 6'4" and over 250 pounds in my prime. I was a professional wrestler and a weight-lifter, and I had been training in judo and jujitsu for some time. But I kept the brochure anyway and something seemed to be telling me to go.

When the time came, I brought twenty of my guys with me, and we watched everyone attacking Professor Jay—choking him, grabbing him, throwing punches—and they were just dropping and tapping left and right. I said to myself, "These guys are just falling down for him. They're with him. There's no way he'd do that to me!" So when he asked for another volunteer, I stepped up. As soon as I went to choke him, ***BOOM***, he had me in a finger lock! I couldn't move! Next he told me to grab him by the wrist, and ***BANG***, he flung me down and had another finger lock on me! No matter what I tried, there was nothing I could do! It was like voodoo! As big and strong as I was, he was *playing* with me.

When it ended, I went back to my students and told them, "This guy is the real deal!" I couldn't move! He was so fluid with his movement. And he never even broke a sweat. Right then and there I realized that I needed to put this in my system. That's when I locked arms with him, and that's when it all started. I immediately bonded with him, and right away we started attending clinics with each other.

SELF-DEFENSE

Self-defense applications and training are vital. I spend a lot of time practicing real-world scenarios—robberies and other kinds of attacks, standing up, against a wall, sitting down, and so on... These encounters are won or lost in the first few seconds, so you have to react right away. Reaction time is everything! If someone comes up and grabs you, you don't ask them what they want—you immobilize them immediately, and **then** ask them what they want. Once my students have this part of their training down, I have them practice blindfolded, so they can learn to react by touch, and I also train them in how to deal with two-on-one situations.

Before meeting the Professor, I only focused on self-defense. He was the one who encouraged me to enter my students into all available divisions at tournaments. I did, and my guys swept the whole thing! Professor Jay would stand there watching with his arms crossed, so proud. As Professor Jay used to say: "We don't brag; we just confess that we're good!" Another thing that is great about Professor Jay's system is that you can teach it to women and children, and they can make the techniques work in a real-life, self-defense situation.

Early on in life I had a stutter and was recovering from polio. The martial arts helped me a lot with this. My father—who was also a wrestler—got me started on this path, but he wasn't around too much, and I lost him at an early age. Well, Professor Jay became like a second father to me. Over the years, I would talk to him every week. He always helped to guide me along the way, and I always give him credit for what I do...

WEAPONS

Any style that doesn't include weapons defense—club, knife, gun—is an incomplete system. In this day and age, you *have* to know how to disarm. And it shouldn't start at black belt—what a waste of time—you need to spend as much time as you can working on these things. My students learn how to deal with weapons right from the start. They learn to respond right away, to close, to take space, to shut down, and to immobilize.

Over the years, I've seen a lot of people play-acting with weapons. What they're doing just wouldn't work on the street. I try to show people the right way to deal with these kind of attacks. After meeting Professor Jay, I immediately added his *kote gaeshi*, goose neck, finger lock, and palming finger, into my weapons disarms and they work beautifully...

Professor Wally Jay was so smart, so kind. He changed my system completely. He is truly missed. In my classes, we always end by bowing to him. He was an icon. When he was in his early nineties, he was *still* able to play with me! Leon Jay is just like his father. It's like with me and my son— Mike—he's been training with me for thirty-five years since he was eight or nine years old. He moves like I do, and is just as good as me, if not better!

—Dave Castoldi, 7th Dan

THE UNDERGROUND ARTS

When I first met Remy Presas, the Filipino fighting arts were largely still underground in the United States—not being taught openly. I was one of the first to invite Remy to teach a seminar and I think he was surprised at how little of Filipino fighting systems was known in America. Like many Filipino arts, his system focused on the flow—"agos"—flowing from strike to strike; from lock to lock; from escape to escape...

—Guro Dan Inosanto

XVI. FREE FIGHTING:
The Delivery System

Whether competing for trophies in tournaments (like those described above) or fighting for your life in the street, the fact remains that when combat is not choreographed, many of the rules you *think* you know go right out of the window! When confronted with the real-world challenges of sweat-slick skin, shortness of breath, and adrenaline-induced agitation, some of the fancier and more experimental tools in the martial armamentarium must give way to simpler, tried-and-true methods.

Grandmaster Leo Fong—the founder of Wei Kuen Do, and another of Professor Wally's colleagues in the council of masters—often emphasizes the combat-effectiveness of mastering a handful of relatively straightforward techniques rather than attempting to amass a vast array of potentially unworkable materials. He teaches that pressure points are the 'targets' of martial arts practitioner, and the various striking methods are the 'delivery system.' It is not surprising, therefore, that many of the basic punches and kicks commonly employed in Wei Kuen Do also comprise an important part of the Small Circle syllabus.

·◊· PROFESSOR BRAD BURGO ·◊·

COMPETITIONS WITH COACH WALLY

Professor Wally Jay: My Judo/Jujitsu training with Professor Wally Jay started in 1959 at the age of five. My father—Walter Burgo—and Professor Jay were friends in Honolulu in the late 1930s, and he was Professor Jay's first assistant coach at the "Kalihi Jujitsu Club." My mother and Bernice Jay were childhood friends and went to grade school together. We followed Professor Jay and his family to Northern California in 1955 and lived upstairs from the Jays and the dojo. This is where Leon Jay and I started our training together.

Start With The Basics: From the first time I stepped onto the mat in 1959 at five years old, our first exercises were always—without fail—wrist extensions and pivoting (including hip action for defense), which completed our three main components (wrist, pivot, and hip action) leading up to the activation or explosion of a throw. Professor Jay implemented the wrist, pivot, and hip action to the movement which required posture, position and perfect balance against your opponent. He required perfection! Every warmup exercise we performed at the start of class had everything to do with Judo or Jujitsu—we never did pushups, jumping jacks, sit-ups, etc... Professor Jay [Wally] would tell us to do those exercises on our own: Our total class time was dedicated to direct knowledge of Judo and Jujitsu.

85

First Principles: At that time, Professor Jay was still working on his innovations (not yet called Small Circle Principles at the time). He used hand-art techniques, chokes, and arm-bars to demonstrate examples. Students often focused on the hand-arts when what he wanted them to focus on were the Small Circle Principle and how to innovate using the principles in their own art or techniques.

During his travels and seminars, Professor Jay taught how to combine and coordinate total body movement using his principles for Judo techniques. In our Judo training for throwing techniques, the mat became the "base," and the total body became the "fulcrum and lever." Then the activation of the throw occurred.

Boxing: At the early age in our Judo and Jujitsu instructions, Professor Jay taught us boxing: Everything from balance, defense, footwork, stability, movement (**mobility**), to punching techniques. Professor Jay loved boxing and how he could innovate using it in Judo and Jujitsu. For instance, he would implement a right cross punch movement and then explain a right side Judo throw using the same movements.

Balance: Principle #1 (balance) was Professor Jay's priority—Maintain perfect balance 100% of the time. When you have perfect balance, posture, and position, it gives you maximum performance which allows you to attack, retreat, defend, re-set, counter, and execute multiple combinations in less than a second.

The Setup: Professor Jay's objective for his students in the 'setup' was to weaken the opponent's position, which in turn strengthened their position and gave them better odds going forward. I would say I learned this from him. Being detail-oriented was one of Professor's great traits. Judo throws are very dynamic, and quite complicated to execute against a knowledgeable opponent. If you fail to give your opponent the very slight action that generates a reaction that you can intercept in order to take control, you have no business advancing to the second step. It was for Professor Jay to notice when a student was trying to execute a throw without employing the first step. He demanded perfection.

Preparation: My favorite trait of Professor's was preparation. He believed that preparation was everything. He explained that without preparation, there is a good chance of failing when executing a technique.

Other Sayings: So many of Professor Jay's beliefs and quotes have stuck with me ever since I was a kid. Here are a few to keep in mind when you are learning, training or teaching:

○ There's no substitute for (perfect) practice.

○ It's all about preparation.

○ Accuracy is so important—be accurate or you are wasting your time.

○ Work smart, not hard—you *can* enter a building through a window, but it is *easier* through the front door.

○ Innovate: You can't fight World War II with World War I weapons/ I enjoyed my model-T Ford, but I like my new car with air-conditioning!

Competitions: When we were kids, Professor Wally Jay took Leon and me everywhere he went. Through the years, he would load up his station wagon and take a car-full of kids to martial arts competitions everywhere, sometimes on several weekends in a row. Our team loved walking into the gymnasium where the competition was being held: the Professor would walk in with his suit and tie, flanked on both sides by his students. We were so proud of him. We thought that he was the classiest coach there.

The Voice: During competition, you could always zero in on his quiet voice when he was coaching us from the side of the mat. He would just use key phrases like: "Circle to your left," or "On your toes." We all listened to him—we knew we could trust him. There were many coaches who would yell instructions to their students the whole time. The Professor would joke with us: "He should have taught his students that in class last week!" He had so much patience with us. When one of us executed a great throw, though, we could hear him shouting above the whole crowd. He let everyone know.

Evolution: Professor Wally Jay would always tell us: "If you are teaching the same things twenty years from now that I am teaching you today, then you have learned nothing, and I was not a good teacher." Over time, I have changed a lot of things that Professor Jay taught me because I have found better ways. Professor Leon Jay has done the same thing as well. But Professor Wally Jay's fundamentals and principles remain the same and will always be the starting point when I examine techniques.

G.O.A.T.: Every one of my team-mates agrees that Professor Wally Jay was the greatest coach—and human being—of all time. We all miss him. When we see each other nowadays, the subject is always our G.O.A.T. (greatest of all time): Coach Wally.

—Brad Burgo, 7th Dan

Hand Techniques	Leg Techniques
Kizamizuki (jab)	*Maegeri* (front kick)*
Gyakuzuki (cross or reverse punch)	*Yokogeri* (side kick)*
Urazuki (uppercut)	*Mawashigeri* (roundhouse kick)
Kagizuki (hook punch)	*Ushirogeri* (back kick)
Uraken (backfist)	*Ushiromawashigeri* (hook kick)
Tettsui (hammerfist)	*Hizauke* (knee check)
Shuto (knife hand)	*Fumikomi* (knee stomp)
Teisho (palm heel)	*Hizageri* (knee strike)
Haito (ridge hand)	*Heisokugeri* (twist kick)
Empi (elbow strike)	*[*Keage/Kekomi* (snap/thrust)]

INTERNAL TECHNIQUES

At higher levels, Small Circle practitioners are taught more complex striking methods, many of which involve the generation or application of internal energy, known as *'ki'* or *'chi'*, as is often seen in certain styles of kung fu. See, for example, "whiplash striking".

Techniques	Effect
Koken (wrist strike)	Channels energy through whiplash
Ipponken (index knuckle)	Focuses energy to smallest point
Nakadakaken (mid-knuckle fist)	Focuses energy to smallest point
Gatsunte (dead hand)	Channels internal energy into strike
Nagashizuki (floating hand)	Gathers and transfers energy
Hiraken (raking knuckle)	Disrupts opponent's energy flow

XVII. SMALL CIRCLE JUDO:
The Art and the Way

Throws are among the most difficult and dangerous techniques in the martial artist's armamentarium.

◊ **Difficulty:** While it is sometimes possible to haul the opponent over the shoulder, like a sack of potatoes, when executed properly, throws can be used to move large opponents great distances with minimal effort.

◊ **Danger:** A bad landing from a fall can be fatal. In 1996, for example, a career criminal attacked a blind man on the streets of Philadelphia. The blind man executed a shoulder throw in self-defense, and the attacker died from the fall.

◊ **Terminology:** While the term: *tori*—the one who takes—is sometimes used to describe the partner who executes the technique in other places in this work, in the context of throws, the more precise term: *nage*—the one who throws—is employed.

◊ *Kuzushi*/**Gripping Up:** In the study of Small Circle Jujitsu, watching video of Professor Leon executing throwing techniques (frame-by-frame if at all possible) is instructive. In conjunction with establishing his grip on the opponent, usually at the lapel and opposite sleeve, the master will apply subtle pressure, pushing or pulling to begin to break the balance.

> ◊ **Tsukuri/Entry:** Likewise, paying close attention to the entry will reveal the way in which this ostensibly preparatory action in fact continues to destroy uke's balance and posture, while at the same time placing nage in the most stable and advantageous position to complete the technique (*kake*), typically with little or no undue effort.

·◊· PROFESSOR DAVE QUINONEZ ·◊·

Historically speaking, Professor Wally Jay's martial arts teachings are based on the jujitsu teachings of Professor Henry Okazaki and the judo training he received from Kenneth Kawachi. Small Circle Judo is a modification of traditional Kodokan Judo. Professor Wally Jay was not afraid of changing techniques to produce faster, more efficient ones. It did not matter to him where the inspiration for the changes came from as long as it produced positive results. This openness to change was one of his greatest assets. He often preached to us that if we were not open to changing how we did something, we might not grow to our full potential. One of his most consistent modifications was to incorporate rotational energy and movement.

If you are familiar with Small Circle Jujitsu you should be aware of the Ten Basic Principles which permeate Professor Wally Jay's jujitsu. It should come as no surprise that it permeated his style of judo as well. The incorporation of the Professor's wrist movements helped to facilitate the magnification of energy we would eventually transmit to—and through—our opponents. On a larger scale we would teach our bodies to take advantage of the effects of these wrist motions and extend them into our throwing techniques, producing what many fondly called "Wally Jay Judo."

In order for these motions to be effective, you must cultivate a firm grip. Without a firm grip, you can try to employ many forces to create an advantage, but you will only pull yourself apart from your opponent, unable to hang on, and as a result, you will be unable to move him in the desired direction. This "truth" was reinforced in my teacher's consciousness by an old judo player—Yuzo Koga—with whom I recently had the privilege of conversing for several hours while attending a local judo tournament.

KOGA SENSEI

Sensei Koga is quite diminutive—less than 110 pounds—and he was my judo idol as a teenager while growing up under Professor Wally Jay's tutelage. At the end of each tournament it was common for Sensei Koga to put on an exhibition consisting of ten matches against ten of the local black belt place winners, one right after the other. In these individual matches, he would always be victorious and never in a small way. He would start with players his size and eventually be pitted against some 200 plus pound giants, and he would crush them with dynamic and awe-inspiring techniques.

While speaking with him, I noticed that he continuously flexed and extended a small grip-exerciser apparatus. When he noticed my line of vision, he apologized for "working out" while we spoke, stating, "It is really important for my judo that I have a very strong grip," to which I replied with one of Professor Wally Jay's many mantras: "A martial artist is always practicing… Always!" Here, a judo legend reminded me through his actions that the small things matter! A true martial artist lives his art.

TAI OTOSHI: A CASE STUDY

Let us take, for example, one of the forward throws: *tai otoshi*.

Rotation: We will utilize a reverse pivot to place our body in the same direction of the throw.

Lean: We will 'induce' gravity as previously mentioned.

Direction: Throwing a right side *tai otoshi* from a right-hand grip mandates that we pull our opponent toward his forward right-hand corner.

Kuzushi: We begin by simultaneously stepping forward with our right foot (toward uke's right foot), while lifting our left arm with a triceps pull at about shoulder height, while at the same time performing an outward rotational wrist action with the left wrist. At the same time, we begin our right arm pull by rotating our right wrist and hand, still gripping uke's collar, toward uke's centerline, finishing with our right hand tightening into a fist and projecting itself in the direction of uke forward right corner. With the tension now firmly pulling both the sleeve arm and the collar, we begin our lean by placing our left foot beside our own right foot, keeping our head and shoulders away, and letting our rotating body break uke's balance, while doing a 180 degree turn. If done correctly, our upper body mass rotation aids in pulling uke forward without utilizing much biceps or triceps contraction. If we add in our biceps and triceps pull, we will appear to be stronger than we really are due to the physics of the centrifugal force about the rotation of our bodies.

Tsukuri: Assuming we have properly bent our knees in order to place ourselves below uke's center of gravity, we are now in a potentially explosive position, ready to ignite at the moment of contact with our partner's body.

Kake: The wrist actions breaks uke's inertia, while the rotation of the reverse pivot helps pull him off balance. That, coupled with the gravity lean, accelerates us at 9.8 meters per second squared (gravitational acceleration)! At the moment our rotating body makes contact with uke's body, we explode out of the runner's stance that is tai otoshi's final leg placement. When we do, we break any remaining inertia, and lift uke by the quick flexion of the ankles (similar to a wrist rotation), immediately followed by the thrust of our leg muscles for maximum lift in the direction of the lean induced moments earlier. If done correctly the speed and power of these actions seems effortless, as we have coupled them synergistically with leverage, rotational momentum, and gravitational forces, which are often underutilized in our sport!

The 'Lean': In order for me to pull or move an opponent without using only my limited muscular strength, I try to utilize the force of gravity (which is available to everyone). To do this, I must be agile and quick to respond at the moment of 'inducement' to apply the throwing technique in line with the gravitational force induced. You can get a clearer sense of what I am suggesting by holding fast to your partner at arm's length and then stepping forward (toward them) while keeping your head and upper body at arm's length, producing your 'lean.' Instantly, you will feel your upper body falling away from your partner, and you will most likely tighten your grip so as not to fall away from them, like a chopped tree as it falls to the ground. This coupling will then induce your partner, almost instantaneously, through the effect of gravity pulling them into the lean as well. In this way, you have let gravity make it appear that you are stronger than you really are. It is pure physics. At the moment of the inducement of forces, you need only apply a throwing technique in the direction of the lean, adding your own strength, to quicken and enhance the application.

But wait you can appear even stronger! Here is where the rotational energy of the wrist can be harnessed effectively. Remembering that if we have trained our wrists to move appropriately, in a dynamic way, we need only apply rotation in the proper direction to enhance 'kuzushi.'

All of these motions and concepts were inspired by Kenneth Kawachi Sensei's fantastic use of his hands and wrists, refined by Professor Wally Jay, and taught to those of us who were fortunate and proud to be his students. The quick snapping of the wrists in rotational motion, focused to the moment of contact, guided along the path of the lean, makes an unstoppable dynamic throw that is as fun to perform as it is to witness. Watching a great throw was one of Professor Wally Jay's great joys during competitions. For us, the greatest joy was watching him responsively blast out of his coach's chair, grinning from ear to ear, eyes twinkling, exclaiming: *"Woo hoo!"* We were all so fortunate to have been taught and influenced by such a wonderful human being and martial artist…

—David Quinonez, 7th Dan

> ○ **Small Circle Practice Pointer:** At a recent seminar in London honoring Professor Wally, Professor Quinonez described the 'lean' as: "Getting your opponent to hop onto your back, allowing the slightest pull or turn of your body to throw him."

XVIII. NECK WORK:
Neck Restraints & Escapes

Small Circle Jujitsu students are not taught neck restraints and escapes until they have achieved a degree of familiarity with both the mechanics and the ethos of the art. This is so because neck restraints are among the most dangerous and potentially deadly techniques in the martial armamentarium. As far back as the dawn of human history, there was no more primal way of extinguishing a life than wrapping the hands around the adversary's throat and quite literally choking life out of him. As a result, such techniques are off limits until the practitioner has achieved fifth *kyu* (green belt).

One of the reasons that neck restraints are so effective is that a number of vital systems run through the neck, and certain types of attack are designed to target each, or sometimes several of these in combination.

Given the extreme danger inherent in employing techniques of this nature, Small Circle practitioners are discouraged from employing them in earnest—even in training—focusing instead on how best to avoid, neutralize, and/or escape from them.

◊ **Blood Choke:** If the opponent cannot think, he cannot fight. A blood choke interrupts or blocks the flow of blood through the carotid arteries/jugular veins. Full occlusion on both sides will typically result in unconsciousness in approximately seven seconds.

◊ **Air Choke:** If the opponent cannot breathe, he cannot fight. An air choke interrupts or blocks the flow of air through the windpipe. Depending when in the respiratory cycle this technique is applied, unconsciousness will typically result in a minute or two, but pain compliance is virtually immediate.

◊ **Nerve 'Choke':** If the opponent cannot control his body, he cannot fight. A nerve 'choke'—which is not, strictly speaking, a true choke—causes spasms by stimulating the vagus nerve. This response is more-or-less instantaneous.

·◊· TONY MAYNARD ·◊·

I started training with Professor Wally Jay in 1984. I met him at the first World Jujitsu Championship in St. Catherine's, Ontario, Canada. I was third degree black belt at the time under Gary Turner of the American Jujitsu Association. I had been invited to compete in this tournament and Wally was the Technical Director. One evening he came into the same restaurant where my wife and I were having dinner, and we invited him to join us. We got to talking and hit it off right away. He was very much a gentleman. I invited him to come in and do a clinic at our school, and later asked him to become my teacher. He agreed. He told me, "A lot of people ask me to be their teacher, but with you, I will..." After that, I would bring him out to our school in North Carolina a couple of times a year, and I would also travel to California to train with him. In time, he told me that he wanted me to become one of his instructors in Small Circle.

"THE BEAR"

Sometime in the mid-1970s, I was teaching a class in Greensboro, North Carolina, and someone there told me that he had just been at an event in Winston-Salem where he had wrestled with a bear! He told me that he had only lasted five seconds with the animal, and he didn't believe that any human being would stand a chance against the animal. Well I was young and stupid, so I said, "Hell, *I'll* wrestle that bear!" So a bunch of us went over to Winston-Salem to take a look.

Thing I did was to *watch*: the bear came out on another guy and it just took him right down—mashed him into the floor! When it was *my* turn, the bear came up and tried to put his weight on me. Well I slipped a little, but when he tried to lay on me, I pushed against him with my back and rolled out from underneath him. As I came out, I caught his head as it was going down. I got my arms around his neck, shot my legs underneath, and flipped him over on his back—the owner was furious! He told me to get out because I was ruining the show for everyone. But on the way out he must have thought better of it because he said to me: "Actually, I have *another* bear you could wrestle..."

Some of the most effective techniques for subduing an opponent are chokes and strangles. I consider any technique that blocks the airway to be a *choke*, and any technique that interrupts the blood-flow to be a *strangle*. Both of these are good ways to get control of an opponent without taking too much of a risk of doing serious damage. In self-defense, people don't like feeling pressure against their neck. It tends to adjust their attitudes real quick! And it allows you to control people. This is important, because in this day and age, you need to be able to account for what you do after the fact, maybe even in a court of law.

Military and civilian are really two different kinds of combat. I have taught in both of these environments. In war, your mission is to finish the enemy, with no time for niceties. In civilian life—even police work—the goal is to *control* the opponent. That is why I have come to focus on control in recent years. You can always escalate if you need to, but you need to maintain control at all times. If you need to let 'the beast' out, it should be like flipping on a light switch (and then flipping it off again). But guys who go for maximum impact straight out of the gate—they are liable to find themselves getting sued. Small Circle is what allowed me to develop very good, humane, controlling techniques. In this art, you can be in agonizing pain one minute, and back to normal the next!

THE <u>SECOND</u> BEAR!

The first bear I wrestled was about five hundred and fifty pounds. The second was more like *nine* hundred, and *ten* feet tall when standing on his hind legs. It took about six months to put that event together. They set up a ring with ropes and hog-wire at a nearby shopping mall. Well I climbed in with that critter and couldn't even get my arms around his neck! He started shaking me and eventually threw me down. When I hit the deck, I realized that I had something in my hands. It was his muzzle (which had come off)! Then the bear opened his mouth and started coming down at me, growling, so I kicked him, but when I did, my foot went right into his mouth! I thought to myself, "Well son, you done got your foot bit off now!" But I kicked with my other leg, and jerked my foot out! Try as I might, though, I could not throw that animal. So when it comes to wrestling with bears, I am one-and-one...

I also believe that simple moves are the most effective. Fancy just isn't going to work when you are sweaty, bloody, or pumped full of adrenaline. My martial arts techniques are field tested. I was also a certified hand-to-hand combat instructor for the United States Navy, so I have a pretty good sense of what works in the real world. The simpler, the better, in my opinion. Even though Small Circle employs many small movements, it still works in real situations.

GOOD TIMES

In 1986, I coached the U.S. Jujitsu team in the World Championships in London, England. We had a great time over there. In 1987, we had the British team come over to the U.S. to compete. Wally was always involved in these exchanges. In 1988, we went to Australia together. In 1989, we had a Canadian team come to North Carolina for a competition. It so happened that the night before this competition, Winston-Salem got hit by tornadoes. There were trees down, and flooding everywhere. Well, Wally and Bernice (his wife) were riding in my van, and we hit some deep water, which flooded out the vehicle. When we got out, the Professor told me, "I can't swim!" So I ended up carrying him and his wife out of the flood waters on my back!

I have blended Small Circle Jujitsu with my American Combat Jujitsu. The Professor used to say that you could blend his system in with what you already do, and that's exactly what I did. And he liked what I was doing. I have also had the opportunity to train with Leon on several occasions over the years. I can tell you that he is a very effective practitioner, and he is worthy to be the Grandmaster of Small Circle Jujitsu. The fact of the matter is that the Small Circle principles are far superior to most of what is out there today. This is Professor Wally Jay's legacy, and I have endeavored to carry on that legacy...

—Tony Maynard, 7th Dan

IXX. LOCKS:
Kansetsu Waza

WRIST LOCKS

Wrist locks are the ideal techniques with which to begin to explore the principles of Small Circle Jujitsu.

◊ **Accessibility:** The wrist is a *small* enough joint that it can be manipulated with relative ease, even by a beginner.

◊ **Safety:** At the same time, the wrist is *large* enough to withstand a fair amount of wear-and-tear as newcomers learn to fine tune their techniques.

◊ **Utility:** Since the hand is the weapon of first resort (and for some, the only weapon in the arsenal), learning to manipulate the joint to which it is attached is one of the most important tools available to those who wish to learn how to defend themselves.

◊ **Evolution:** The overall directions for the application of most wrist locks can be easily demonstrated and understood using the large motions (big circles) commonly employed in the classical era. As the practitioner gains experience, however, she learns the power of tracking tighter, more effective arcs (small circles and spirals) in executing these same techniques.

◊ **Principles and Precepts:** While the practitioner should seek to apply as many of the Small Circle Principles and Precepts as possible in the execution of *every* technique, certain wrist locks lend themselves very well to illustrating particular concepts, such as the importance of aiming toward the centerline when applying the Bent Elbow Wrist Lock, the value of **two-way action** in amplifying the effect of the Chicken Wing, or the power of spiral motion in performing and maintaining the Vertical Lock.

ARM & SHOULDER LOCKS

In a syllabus comprising roughly one hundred core techniques, arm and shoulder locks account for almost a fifth of them. The reason for this is simple: In the heat of an actual engagement, the precise coordination required to execute certain complex moves can be a hard commodity to come by. As a result, the practitioner is forced to rely on gross motor movements applied to larger targets like the arm.

Arm and shoulder locks have several advantages:

◊ **Grip:** Particularly if skin is slick with sweat or blood, it can be hard to obtain and retain a hold on various body parts, but the wrist provides a perfect gripping-point under almost any conditions. In addition, the wrist is a veritable treasure-trove of pressure points.

◊ **Control:** Locking the arm automatically takes one of the opponent's most powerful weapons off the table, and, if done correctly, can often impede an attack from the other arm, or even control the entire body.

◊ **Effect:** The arm/shoulder joints are large enough that their immobilization can effectively neutralize the opponent's entire body, but not so large as to be too difficult to manipulate.

FINGER LOCKS

There can be no doubt that when properly applied—that is to say escape-proofed and sufficiently intensified—finger locks are fight-enders. No matter how strong and flexible the adversary, a finger will inevitably bend and break if sufficient force is applied. The key question, then, is not how to *apply* these techniques, but rather, how to *access* them; in other words, how to get hold of the finger in the first place!

◊ **Prying Entry (Fist):** Given the relative weakness of any individual finger in relation to the strength of a hand, it is often possible to pry one or more digit loose from a striking or grabbing fist.

◊ **Pocket Entry (Open Hand):** One of the easiest ways to get hold of a finger is to maneuver the body in such a way as to create a pocket of empty space under one or more digits, as in the case of twisting the torso in response to an open handed push or pin.

◊ **Reactive Entry (Pressure Point):** Another useful access method, either alone or in conjunction with others, is to strike, rub, or otherwise activate release points on the hand or arm that typically cause the opponent's grip to open.

◊ **Fortuitous Entry (Grappling):** One of the most rewarding access methods, particularly when grappling, is simply to wait for a finger to 'present itself' by happenstance, which tends to happen with surprising reliability.

○ **Small Circle Practice Pointer:** When employed correctly (escape-proof, maximum pain without dislocation), finger-locks are fight-enders!

In 1987, I moved to Boston and, to my great fortune, stumbled into the West Newton YMCA to investigate the Jujitsu classes being taught there. I had been training in the martial arts for ten years and held a First Degree Black Belt in Jujitsu. With additional training in Karate and Judo—and approaching my physical prime—I felt like a pretty solid fighter. But I was about to find out what I *didn't* know…

The YMCA was the home to Dave Castoldi's Street Self-Defense Jujitsu School. Dave Castoldi was, at the time, a 6'4", 240 pound, monster of a Boston street-fighter. Many years earlier, Dave had become a loyal follower of Professor Wally Jay and Small Circle Jujitsu. If you want to see something impressive, watch a man of that size—who can move like a big cat—destroy an attacker with unimaginably subtle and controlled fine motor skill techniques.

I remember my first day being thrown into the grinder. My approach, as a "traditional" jujitsu fighter, was to strike, take-down, and strike some more. I was holding my own, but tiring quickly due to the high levels of exertion. After about a dozen attacks followed by throws and more, it was my partner's turn—a welcome change as I was fairly gassed-out.

Harry Curtis was a young Castoldi green belt, much smaller than me. On his first defense, the moment I hit the ground, he pinned my head to the mat with his knee and slapped a finger lock on me. If you have never experienced a finger lock, I can tell you for my part that I have never felt so vulnerable. It was a masterful move, concentrating the attack on the weakest part of my body. Minimal exertion of energy. The technique was such that my efforts to escape only created more pain. "Wow, what was that?" I asked. "Small Circle Jujitsu," they said. "Ever heard of Professor Wally Jay?"

That moment was the biggest game-changer in my now-forty years of martial arts study. In the following years, studying under Professor Castoldi and Professor Jay, I discovered the efficiency and effectiveness of Small Circle Theory combined with practical, street-wise self-defense techniques. My favorite technique of all time is still the *finger lock*—brutal and elegant at the same time. Known to be a fight-stopper and occasional giant-killer.

The power of finger locks lies in their adaptability to different situations. They can be used with restraint, to control an attacker through pain compliance; or abruptly executed, to destroy a joint; or used anywhere along the Control-Destroy continuum as the situation dictates. Finger locks can be used standing or on the ground. They are an effective transition to and from many other joint manipulations, takedowns, and strikes. The finger lock is a fine-motor-skill technique with gross-motor-skill impact.

Making effective use of finger locks requires some skill and understanding of the underlying principles. It requires more than merely grabbing the fingers and bending them back. A properly executed finger lock incorporates a number of Small Circle principles, including:

o Proper Grip: Focusing on placement of the fulcrum and lever in the correct positions on the finger being attacked;

o Two-way Action: Moving the fulcrum and lever in opposite directions and avoiding the head-on collision of force;

o Small Circle Motion: Applying the technique with a small, ever-tightening, circular action.

When executed properly, finger locks can be effective self-defense weapons for people of all sizes and martial arts styles. That is what I learned the first day I met Dave Castoldi—just as he learned the first day he met Wally Jay (there is a good story behind that, as well). Practicing finger locks relentlessly has served me well, especially as I get older and am less able to perform with the same physicality as I once could. My banging days are behind me. Efficient pain-compliance and quick finishes go a long way nowadays.

I am so grateful for the discovery of the Small Circle finger lock—a game-changer for me and a technique staple since. Thank you to Professor Wally Jay for selflessly sharing his knowledge, and having such a huge impact on me and so many other martial artists around the World. *Aloha!*

—Bill Troy, 6th Dan

○ **Small Circle Practice Pointer:** The devastating power of finger locks is one of the primary reasons that teachers drill into their students the importance of making and maintaining a strong fist. If the natural resting state of the hand is closed, it makes it harder (but certainly not impossible) for the opponent to get hold of a single digit, and thereby, likely end the fight…

XX. GRAPPLING/GROUND WORK:
Katame Waza

Long before ultimate fighting events began broadcasting grappling contests into homes the world over, students of Small Circle Jujitsu were training to ensure that they could apply these techniques both on their feet and on the ground with equal effectiveness. There are many reasons that the total warrior should strive to ensure that this aspect of training is not neglected:

◊ **Grappling Safety:** Engagements involving more wrestling techniques than boxing blows tend to be safer for those involved, primarily because they usually involve less striking, particularly to the head and neck.

◊ **Going to Ground:** The majority of street fights end up with one or both combatants on the ground at some point. As a result, being able to operate in this 'horizontal' environment is critical to any system of self-defense.

◊ **The Equalizer:** While there are some opponents who are more dangerous on the ground than in a stand-up fight, this tends to be the exception, not the rule. Accordingly, going to the ground will often work to the Small Circle practitioner's advantage.

◊ **Submission:** Ground-fighting offers a wide variety of ways of neutralizing the opponent, or forcing him to submit, under controlled conditions, thereby reducing physical—and legal—risk.

◊ **Weapon Control:** When weapons are involved, much of the calculus of free-fighting is altered significantly. Gaining control of the weapon becomes the paramount concern, and pinning the limb in which that weapon is being held is a great place to start.

◊ **Entries:** Whether fighting on the ground, on one's feet, or even, as is so often the case in real-word combat, some combination of the two, the quality of the entry is very much determinative of the degree of difficulty—or even viability—of the technique that follows. In this respect, the Small Circle grappling and groundwork arena is an ideal crucible in which to refine this vital skill.

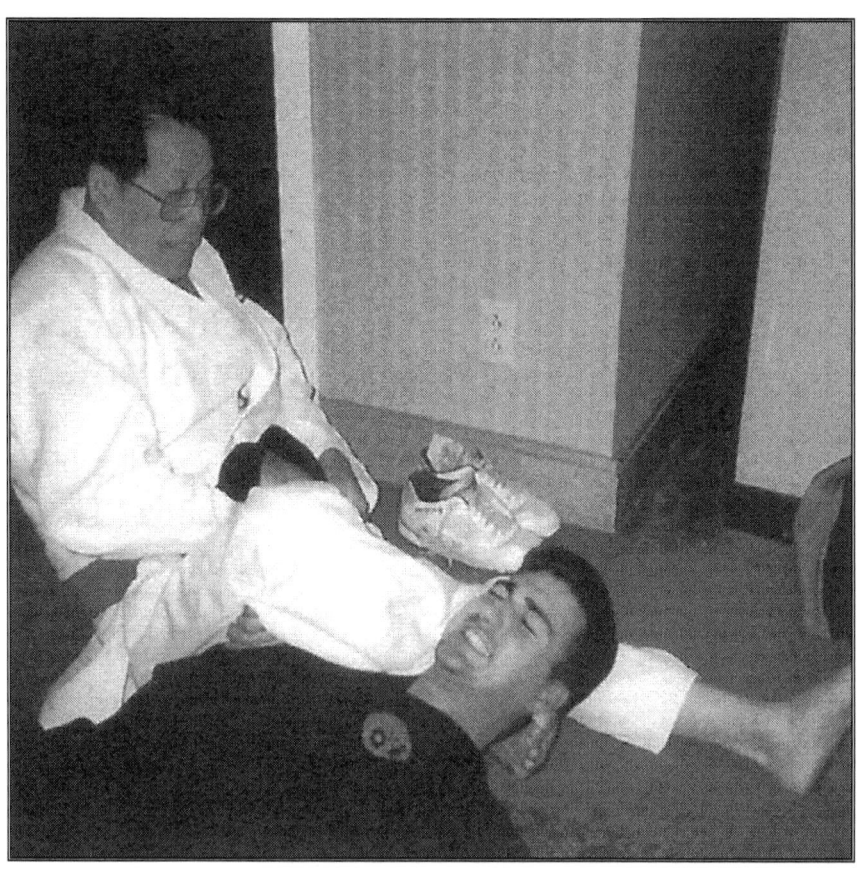

·◇· John Mellon ·◇·

Entry Skills & Methodology

Professor Leon and I were tasked to work on a couple of revisions of the syllabus during the last decade or so of his father's life. Professor Wally had made me his Technical Adviser (to my complete bafflement) in the mid-1990s, and I was there mostly to act as a convenient sounding-board for Professor Leon. The small contribution I made was to bring the perspective of a multi-disciplinary stylist to the overall structure of the syllabus and to add some continuous cyclical drilling, with an emphasis on entering techniques.

Both for the purpose of getting initial contact and control of the opponent, and for offering a reference framework to guide the stylist in choosing the most efficient and immediate technical response, it is important to understand and recognize instantly what opportunity is presented by that first touch. This is usually what is able to be applied with the least amount of adjustment from the first contact, and it fulfils Professor Wally's concern for efficiency and is integral to what we each understood as combative flow.

I routinely teach some simple drills to the seniors for the purpose of sharpening their entry skills. Some are taken directly from the Southeast Asian arts of *Kalis*, *Silat*, and *Kuntao*, and some are heavily amended for the purposes of my own students and those of Small Circle. All are constructed in such a way as to improve both technical performance and combative attributes.

—John Mellon, 7th Dan

LINEAR 4-COUNT DRILL

1. Uke punches with RH, tori **parries** inward with LH.

2. Tori's RH comes from below to **control** uke's arm.

3. Tori's LH **clears** uke's arm to make way for RH strike.

4. Pattern switches: Uke parries, controls, clears, counters...

ENTRY #1: CHECKING

1 &2. For Entry #1, the first two moves are the same as in the give-and-take drill.

3. The third move is also similar, but entry/clearing is deeper.

4. The deep control turns uke, opening up striking targets.

5. Tori can then transition to a hammerlock (or other finish).

ENTRY #2: TRAPPING

1 &2. For Entry #2, the first two moves are the same as in the give-and-take drill.

3. The third move is modified from a clearing to a clockwise pass.

4. Tori then feeds uke's wrist into his L elbow and traps it.

5. Tori can then transition to an arm bar (or other finish).

FEDERAL AGENTS

One of the Professor's students who regularly spends time at the government training facilities in Quantico, Virginia, reports that federal agents are increasingly being trained in jujitsu in order to prepare them to assess and neutralize real world threats.

XXI. DEFENSIVE MEASURES:
Body Armor

AGOS—THE FLOW

On a steamy Fourth-of-July weekend, Guro Dan Inosanto—who not only lived through the age when the Eastern fighting arts first flourished on Western shores, but also helped to shape it—kindly took the time to share certain memories of those early days, and to provide some guidance for modern followers of the Way...

·◊· GURO DAN INOSANTO ·◊·

Professor Wally Jay has been one of my heroes since the early days. I first met him when I was training in judo and he was coaching a team in Alameda, California. Around this time, Bruce Lee was training with people like Wally and Gene LeBell, incorporating whatever he found to be useful. I would say that Bruce absorbed a great deal from Wally Jay. He would flow from, say, a boxing combination, into a Wing Chun pattern, into a series of locking techniques, without any noticeable break, weaving it all into a structure that he called "Jun Fan." And he always talked very highly of Professor Jay.

One of the things that was important to both Bruce Lee and Wally Jay was that the art had to work for the individual. Some people learn a system and then practice and teach it the exact same way it was handed down to them. There is nothing wrong with this, but others try to improve the system along the way, and to customize it to make it work for each individual practitioner. Bruce and Wally were both innovators, and both believed that it was vital to individualize the system (I call it "tailoring"). For example, of the sixty-seven odd throws in judo, maybe only two or three will work well for you, but then again, that's all you need to be an effective fighter. In this way, their systems are constantly evolving, both over time and by individual.

Wally Jay was a fair bit older and was something of an idol to me—even more so when I had the chance to train with him. Wally Jay seminars were always among my wife Paula's and my favorites. He really proved his technique by doing. Professor Jay made you a believer very quickly! One of the unique aspects of his art was that the techniques were so painful, but the second you tapped out, the pain was gone, and there was no damage at all. He never broke anyone's limbs, but when he applied a lock, the pain was unbearable! It was like turning on a tap (and then off). Small Circle Jujitsu is an amazing art, and Wally Jay was a true gentleman. Because of his maturity and wisdom, he was the ideal martial role model.

The Greek philosophers taught that the highest form of learning was to teach—when you teach others, you teach yourself—and by that standard, Wally Jay was one of the world's greatest learners as well as teachers. When you teach, you have to be ready for any question, not just your own. To this day, when I learn something, I like to share it with someone else, partly because I enjoy sharing with others, and partly because it helps me to analyze the material. Wally Jay was very big on sharing. He was never secretive or guarded with his techniques.

An important, but often over overlooked aspect, of the martial arts is defense. For a start, you learn a lot by being on the receiving end of technique. One of the things Bruce Lee seemed to like about working with me is that I was durable and able to stand up to all kinds of attacks! And so much of that depends on conditioning. Stamina is just as important—maybe even more so—than more obvious qualities like strength, speed, and agility. Together, these qualities make up the essence of combat, but without conditioning, higher level skills like strategy go right out the window! The body's muscular system plays a very important role in fighting. So does the respiratory system. Sports teams, for example, use all kinds of drills and equipment to help condition their players so that they are able to execute their plays.

Bruce Lee taught his students that they should develop both offensive and counter-offensive [defensive] systems. In addition to being able to launch an effective attack, the well-rounded fighter needs to be ready to nullify any kind of attack, no matter what style the attacker employs. In this way, the defensive component actually needs to be broader than the offensive piece. You need to be able to roll out of a throw, counter a lock, deflect a punch, and so on...

—Guro Dan Inosanto

DEFENSES

Doctors are taught that the first commandment of their profession is to do no harm. Martial arts teachers—at least the good ones—subscribe to this same philosophy. While the utility of a particular technique in a real-world confrontation can be debated, the encumbrance of a training injury cannot. It sidetracks the mind, stalls the body, and blunts the spirit.

It is a standing joke among Small Circle practitioners that the system's bow is performed by flopping one mangled hand lifelessly on top of the other (at least at the end of a class)! But in reality, great care is taken to avoid injuring one another. In fact, one of the first *kyu* tests stresses the importance of understanding how to deal safely with a partner who does not respond to standard methods of applying techniques.[3]

---

3. Recommended responses include **pulsing** and **waving**.

Protecting oneself from injury takes many forms:

○ **Before:** It is important to warm up properly before practice—especially in cold weather—so that muscles become hyperemic; joints, loose; and ligaments, pliable.

○ **During:** When practicing throws, it is vital that each partner knows how to take a fall, just as it is critical when practicing locks that each knows how to signal submission before any real damage is done.

○ **After:** Finally, as discussed elsewhere in this text, such recuperative practices as pressure point resuscitation and restorative massage are extremely important components of the Small Circle syllabus.

Professor Wally sometimes said that throwing the opponent was simply 'hitting him with the ground.' As a result, Small Circle practitioners are taught multiple ways of controlling the damage caused by being 'hit' by such a massive 'weapon'.

○ **Small Circle Practice Pointer:** A throw is like hitting the enemy with the ground!

A. Falls (*ukemi*): One way to minimize the force of the impact of a fall is to spread it across as wide an area as possible. When in such a defensive configuration, the Small Circle practitioner strives to achieve the *opposite* of the offensive principle: **focus energy to the smallest point.**

○ **Spread the Force:** The idea is to make contact with the ground using as much of the body as possible, so as to spread the cumulative force over the greatest area.

○ **Absorb the Shock:** To the extent possible, the body parts that first make contact with the ground should be padded (not bony), and act as shock-absorbers, yielding slightly on impact.

○ **Hit the Ground Back:** In addition, when falling, it is helpful to slap the ground sharply in order to dissipate the energy even further (the harder the slap, the more energy it takes from the fall, as well as directing that energy in the opposite direction). At more advanced levels, the same effect can be achieved with less risk to the hand by simply pulsing the muscles.

○ **Rocking:** While a break*fall* is not a roll, it can still borrow some of the value of the *kaiten ukemi* (roll) by arcing the contact limbs slightly (think of rocking chair skids).

B. Rolls (*kaiten ukemi*): In order to avoid head-on collision with the ground altogether, Small Circle practitioners are taught to roll whenever possible. Sometimes the force of the throw is too great, or the angle is too steep, to allow time to tuck and roll, but when it is possible to translate linear momentum into **rotational momentum**, it is a very powerful defensive measure. When doing so, however, it is vital to roll on the shoulder, not the head or neck. And because of the myriad directions in which one can be thrown, it is important to learn how to roll forwards, backwards, and to either side.

COLLABORATION AND ESCAPE

To the uninitiated, the breakfalls and rolls can appear staged in the sense that *uke* appears to be cooperating with *nage's* technique. Once the process is properly understood, however, it becomes clear that *ukemi* are often techniques for *escaping* from a far worse fate, like a broken arm, a close-quarters exchange of blows, or just a hard fall. Using these methods, people have survived jumping from fast moving vehicles and falling from great heights. They are certainly sufficient to minimize the impact of even an expertly-executed throw.

○ **Small Circle Practice Pointer:** The earth is your friend—you can use it to ground yourself when under attack...

XXII. THE NEXT LEVEL:
Densho

Following the watershed British victory in the Second Battle of El Alamein in 1942, Sir Winston Churchill famously quipped: *"Now this is not the end. It is not even the beginning of the end. But it is, perhaps, the end of the beginning..."*

Mastering the techniques described in this work is not the end of the Small Circle journey. It is not even the beginning of the end. But it is, perhaps, the end of the beginning, for these techniques constitute its core.

There is, however, a wider world to be explored; a broader canvas on which the martial artist can make his mark:

○ **Specialized Techniques:** There are many situation-specific techniques to be absorbed (while *all* techniques are, at least to some degree, dependent on the situation with which the practitioner is confronted, there are a handful of moves in the Small Circle syllabus that are intended for use in very specific circumstances).

These include:

■ **The Four Wrist Escapes:** Thumb-wrist entry; web up; wedge out; and floating elbow;

■ **The Four Leg Takedowns:** Forward shoulder; inside shoulder; forward elbow; and inside elbow.

■ **Come-Alongs:** Reverse finger hammer lock; reverse finger arm bar; outward goose neck; reinforced standing center lock; (several others).

■ **Handshake Variations:** Extended fingers; thumb twist; turning; LI-4 press; (several others).

○ **Densho—"The rest of the story":** While the locks, throws, strikes, neck restraints, grapples, and miscellaneous techniques enumerated in the core curriculum through *ikkyu* are sufficient to meet almost any challenge imaginable, there are countless others—within both the art itself as well as its constituent components—to be discovered absorbed, incorporated, and blended into the organic and ever-expanding universe of Small Circle Jujitsu.

○ **Permutations and Combinations:** Each of the above-referenced core techniques—what we might call the Small Circle Canon—can be broken down into smaller parts or combined into larger sets. In fact, it is the ability to break down and stitch together combinations of techniques seamlessly—**transitional flow**—that marks the master practitioner of this art.

SHODAN, NIDAN, SANDAN, AND BEYOND

The techniques that are referenced in this work comprise the entire Small Circle syllabus through **first *kyu***.

I From **first *kyu*** to **first *dan***, the practitioner is expected to polish these techniques to a degree that is worthy of this rank—to master these basic building blocks—a requirement that is perhaps best tested by a demonstration of **transitional flow** showcasing all aspects of the art.

II By tradition, **second *dan***—which follows after an appropriate number of years of active training and teaching of the art—is the most grueling rank. The *randori* component of this milestone is essentially a punishing endurance test administered by 'a circle of friends!'

III **Third *dan* and beyond:** Beyond these clearly-defined steps, Professor Leon has indicated that contributions to the cause (***koken***)—the development and sharing of new skills and ideas, for example—is the yardstick by which progress in the art of Small Circle Jujitsu is measured. In fact, a special event designed to facilitate this very kind of innovation and exchange among experienced practitioners was held on the East Coast of the United States in 2019 to coincide with, and compliment, the compilation of this work.

It should also be noted that, in rare instances, "field promotions" may be made outside of this technical structure in response to demonstrations of extraordinary fighting or teaching skill exhibited by individual Small Circle Jujitsu practitioners.

○ **Additional Arts:** As various chapters in this work indicate, as Small Circle practitioners advance through the ranks, they learn how to acquire targets like pressure point fighters; how to punch like boxers; how to kick like *karate-ka*; and how to swing the cane like *arnisadors*.

MILESTONES

For a true black belt, knowledge begins to transform into *wisdom* and strength into *power*. A real master adds such attributes as balance (*grace*), agility (*adaptability*), and precision (*judgment*) to the arsenal. And for a genuine grandmaster, the path leads *inward* through many doorways...

·◊· **Dr. Charles M. Terry** ·◊·

Small Circle Jujitsu can be used to enhance any style of martial arts. It provides a comprehensive arsenal of self-defense techniques as well as warm-ups, exercises, principles and drills that can be easily incorporated into every martial arts class. Whether a style focuses on kata, sparring, fitness, competition, or grappling, SCJ can be seamlessly integrated. With both "hard" and "soft" elements, SCJ can be adapted to fit the practitioner and the environment. It is the universal nature of SCJ that has allowed this system to spread across the globe.

Warm-ups: SCJ warm-ups help loosen the muscles, connective tissues, and joints, with a focus on preparation for the practice of locks and throws. A warm-up geared towards SCJ can add variety to the beginning of any martial arts class. The added bonus is that most of the warm-up techniques can be used in self-defense as well. Students are taught to stretch the wrists so as to mimic the goose neck, bent elbow wrist lock, and other wrist locks and throws. The thumb-wrist entry can be used as an entry for chokes, arm bars, and ankle locks. And the wrist-radius exercise can then be applied to increase the effectiveness of these techniques. Wrist extensions help the practitioner ingrain the mindset of the ever-tightening circle and can also help with energy transfer.

Falls and Rolls: Learning to fall and to roll is arguably the most important self-defense technique a practitioner will ever encounter. Everyone has fallen at some time in the past and, assuming gravity persists, is likely to fall again at some time in the future. Falls lead to many injuries in young and old alike, including broken hips, ankles, and arms, as well as more serious spine and head injuries. Classes on falling properly are even taught to senior citizens to reduce the risk of incapacitating or even life-threatening injuries. Professor Leon loves to tell the story of his mother Bernice—in her 80s at the time—falling from the kitchen counter where she had been standing to clean the cabinets, and doing a perfect breakfall before getting right back to work! Stunt men and women learn to fall and roll in order to do amazing athletic feats and remain unscathed, and falls and rolls are fun to practice in class and are great for circulating energy and loosening up the whole body. Rolls can be used as a means of escaping locks, grabs, and throws, and make any demonstration more dynamic. In this manner, rolls can be used in two-person drills to further enhance skills and make class more interesting.

The Principles: The Principles of SCJ are applicable to every style of martial art. They can be used to analyze techniques and improve the skill of practitioners, and they were a godsend when my dojo had to transition to teaching classes online during the COVID pandemic. With no idea how to make online classes interesting and engaging, I decided to pick a theme to focus on each week. Balance (discussed below) seemed like an obvious choice for the first session. It was not until after that class, however, that it dawned on me that I could do the same with all of the SCJ Principles—wiser men than me had already mapped out the next few months of teaching themes for me, and this also allowed me to work the very hands-on art of SCJ into every karate class. When I realized this, I couldn't wait to share this plan with my students and move on to the next week's theme…

Balance: I began by analyzing our basic techniques and coming up with ways to focus on the **balance** component. Balance-kick competitions have long been a staple of our karate classes: The goal is to see who can do the most kicks while standing on one leg. Students who lose their balance are instructed to switch to jumping jacks (on the honor system), which keeps everyone moving—an added bonus for those of us who are allergic to down time! Balance is not limited to kicking techniques however. Instead of performing blocks, punches, and other such basic hand techniques from a traditional *kiba dachi* (horse stance), they can be done while standing on one leg for the first set and then repeated while balancing on the other leg. This not only provides a means of disguising repetition, but also develops balance while making basics more fun and challenging.

Mobility and Stability: As with the yin/yang symbol, **mobility and stability** can be considered opposites. The deeper the stance and wider the base, the more stable it is. This allows more power to be projected into a technique. It also provides a lower center of gravity, which is useful in performing throws. By contrast, higher stances, such as the *neko dachi* (cat stance), allow for quicker responses and changes in position. In our virtual classes we practiced basics from a low *kiba dachi* or *seiuchin* stance, and then practiced quick techniques and transitions from *neko dachi*. This theme also provided a nice platform to discuss yin and yang, which are in constant motion or transition. This is a good analogy for the way in which footwork and stances continually transition during a fight in order to achieve whatever is needed at any given moment. In a more global sense, the COVID pandemic forced us all to develop 'mobility' and flexibility in finding ways to perform essential tasks like distance learning, shopping, and socializing, all while sheltering in our **stable** residences or other places.

Avoid Head-on Collision of Forces: The principle of **avoiding the head-on collision of forces** goes hand-in-hand with mobility and stability. Mobility is required to avoid an attack and deflecting a punch or kick requires far less energy, and is far safer, than meeting an incoming blow head-on. One-step fighting (or combinations as it is sometimes called) is a great training method for this principle. In our preferred method, the "designated hitter" stands in a left foot forward *seisan dachi* (front stance) with the guard up, while the defender stands in a neutral stance, because this more closely simulates what may occur in an actual altercation. The attacker then steps with the right foot and punches with the right hand and the defender blocks/parries/avoids the attack and counters with any technique (hand or leg strikes, joint locks, chokes, or throws). This drill can be expanded in a variety of ways, including having the attacker approach, and the defender evade, along the diagonal, in a manner similar to the "V-step" common in the Filipino arts, or by adding a counter-attack/counter-defense (three step fighting). In all variations on this theme, however, the principle of avoiding the head-on collision of forces is employed.

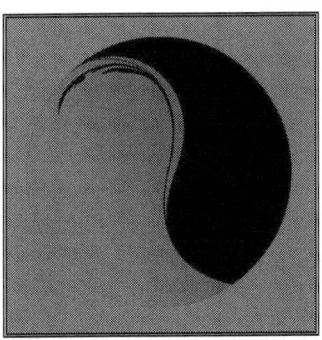

Mental Resistance and Distraction: As anyone who has studied SCJ can attest, one can develop sufficient **mental resistance** to counter just about any lock. However, the **distraction** of a slap across the face, a *kiai*, a kick, or punch can effectively counter even well-honed mental resistance. Throughout classes that focused on this Principle, students were challenged to focus on one task (training in a virtual martial arts class) while blocking out the distraction of siblings, pets wandering through the "workout area," and thoughts of other daily obligations and recreational activities. Practitioners of *Ryukyu Kempo* and certain other styles of karate perform a kata called *Sanchin*. In practicing this form, the student strives to develop a focused mind, body, and spirit. Instructors test the individual's focus by attempting to distract the student with vocal assaults, pushes, feints, strikes, and even boards being broken over their bodies. The goal of the student is to complete the form while remaining focused in the face of adversity. This helps to strengthen focus not just in the martial arts, but also in virtually every other aspect of life as well. A student cannot do well on a math test, for example, while simultaneously worrying about the social studies test that is occurring later that day. A driver cannot effectively and safely drive a car if focused on children fighting in the back seat, the radio, or a cell phone. In an even broader sense, during the COVID pandemic, students struggled to attend to school-work at home despite myriad distractions, and parents had to fill the role of teachers and coaches while at the same time running a household and attempting to work from home. Never was it more important to learn to focus on the task at hand.

Focus to the Smallest Point Possible: It is easier to break a board with a punch than with a slap. Using only two knuckles when punching will **focus even more energy into a smaller area.** In structuring classes around this Principle, students were encouraged to think about each technique. What is the target? What is the striking surface? A well placed punch can break a single rib rather than spreading force across several ribs thereby causing less overall damage. Kicks focused with the ball of the foot or just the heel will have a greater impact than simply slapping the target with the bottom of the foot. And as every SCJ practitioner learns, striking pressure points or vital areas requires precision that is well worth the payoff.

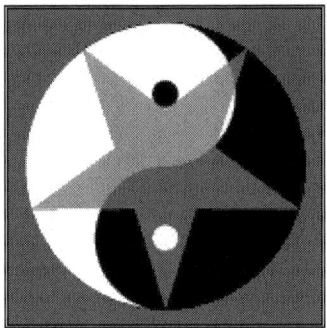

Energy Transfer: **Energy transfer** is one way of breaking an opponent's resistance. It allows the practitioner to apply energy in the most efficient manner possible. After making the initial contact, the point of impact and the surrounding areas become hypersensitive, and thus more susceptible to follow-up attacks. In acupressure terms, striking three points along a meridian will produce an enhanced effect with each blow, as will striking the same point three times. This principle can be applied very effectively in conjunction with **mental resistance and distraction.** When an arm bar is applied to the triceps tendon (TW-11), it creates a "vacuum of energy" further along this same meridian. The opponent's energy becomes focused at TW-11, so by suddenly shifting pressure to the mid-triceps (TW-12), the opponent can be dropped to the floor with very little effort. Professor Wally would often demonstrate this principle by applying pressure below the elbow (between TW-9 and TW-10) using a heavy palm and then transferring energy above the elbow (TW-11). In kata, it is not uncommon for a single point to be struck with **three punches**, as with the three-punch sequence common to many I-pattern forms or the triple punches seen in kata *Seisan* or *Passai*. This pattern can symbolize that the first strike to a given point will produce a certain effect; a second strike to the same spot, with the same power, will produce a greater effect; and a third strike to this same target requires even less effort to produce even greater results. Western boxers have long known that going after the same target on an opponent can produce an enhanced effect. In this way, the principle of energy transfer can be analyzed in class by studying anatomy and acupuncture meridians, and practiced during basics by directing sets of three techniques (whether using the same or different techniques) to the same target.

Fulcrum, Lever, and Base: This Principle provides a means of exploring many different techniques found in karate basics and kata. It can also be seen in the employment of **two-way action**. In virtual classes, students were taught to use their imagination to picture grabbing an opponent with the retracting hand and striking or throwing with the other hand. In this exercise, the retracting hand serves as a **fulcrum**, while the extending hand/arm is used as a **lever**. Similarly, in applying (or imagining applying) leverage in finger locks, the other hand, the body, the leg, a wall, or even a nearby piece of furniture can serve as a **base**.

Sticking Control and Sensitivity: Mastering this Principle requires refining the ability to respond to the partner's/opponent's energy and reacting quickly and smoothly to that energy, with just the right amount of force. When working with a partner, sticking hands drills, slow movements, and open communication can add a new dimension to a practitioner's abilities. The feedback one can obtain from this kind of practice fosters the development of sensitivity to *tactile* cues given by an opponent, and it is awareness of these *tactile* (as opposed to visual) cues that reduces reaction time. Practicing the Principle of **sticking, control, and sensitivity** *without a partner* provides unique challenges, but some of the SCJ warm-ups provide a starting point: In order to loosen the joints, the SCJ student learns to use one hand to manipulate the other into the positions of the goose neck, the wrist lock, the bent-elbow wrist lock, and so on. In addition to loosening the joints and making them better able to withstand the application of these techniques, this exercise also serves to develop sensitivity as one is simultaneously *applying* and *experiencing* each lock. In a similar way, one can work toward developing the kind of sticking sensitivity required to capture the opponent's wrist in any of the four major ways (right hand on right wrist from inside; right hand on left wrist from inside; right hand on right wrist from outside; right hand on left wrist from outside) by practicing positioning one hand at one's own opposite elbow, sliding down toward the wrist while "latching on," and tightening the grip just above the wrist to trap the hand and activate the wrist pressure points. This exercise can be performed on either the palmar or dorsal side of the forearm and with the hand either "web up" or "web down."

Rotational Momentum: As Professor Wally described it, **rotational momentum** involves beginning to throw an opponent by rotating them in one direction, and when resistance is encountered, quickly changing the direction of the throw to move in concert with the opponent's attempts to resist—in essence, "going with the flow" of the opponent's resistance. This Principle is reflected in the saying: *"One cannot resist in more than one direction at the same time,"* and is illustrated in the kata *Kusanku*. There is a sequence in this form where the practitioner stands in a left foot forward stance with hands in a left augmented block position. The practitioner retracts the right hand while sweeping with the left leg and then performs a right-left punch combination. One possible interpretation of this sequence of moves is: Grabbing the opponent for a throw [augmented block—closed fist represents grabbing the opponent]; minor inner/outer reap [foot sweep]; and reversing the initial direction of the throw [double punch—first punch baits, second punch reverses]. This interpretation of rotational momentum can be reinforced in class by practicing basics in sets of two (double punches, double blocks, double chops, etc…). It can also be performed in conjunction with footwork to drill reaps and throws, either with or without a partner. With repetition comes mastery. One can also examine kata for sequences that may represent employing rotational momentum on a single opponent rather than practicing the same technique on both sides. This may, in fact, be one of the reasons that there are so many sequences of three techniques **in** kata: The first represents the application of the initial technique, while the second and third represent resistance and the employment of the principle of rotational momentum in response.

Rotational Momentum II: The Ever-Tightening Spiral: The principle of **rotational momentum** may have had its origin in reversing the direction of throws, but Professor Leon has taken the two-dimensional concept of an ever-tightening *circle* and added the third dimension to create the concept of an **ever-tightening *spiral*.** When this three-dimensional approach is applied to parries and joint locks, the increased effectiveness it yields is readily apparent. Another interpretation of this Principle that has evolved over time is based in physics and relates to the dissipation of stored potential energy when a practitioner is thrown or falls from a standing position to a roll [explored in greater detail in Appendix A]. In this way, practicing rolls in class is an excellent lead-in to a discussion of the principle of rotational momentum.

Transitional Flow: This aspect of SCJ involves moving seamlessly from one technique to another, blending with the partner or opponent's energy in order to maintain control. It combines all the other principles of SCJ and is performed with a partner as a practical exercise. Just as free-sparring is used in karate or tae kwon do to test the student's ability to respond to random attacks, **transitional flow** allows the SCJ practitioner to formulate defenses in an unscripted manner.

As with musical improvisation, the artist may develop "licks" or preferred combinations of techniques which can be adjusted based on the reactions of different training partners. The goal is to be able to respond to any real attack with an arsenal of techniques that flow together naturally. As with half-speed sparring, **transitional flow** may be practiced slowly to find the "holes" in combinations that could allow an opponent to escape. And as with the restrain required in no-contact, or light-contact sparring, transitional flow should be performed in such a way as to create maximum pain—especially during transitions—in order to maintain control, but without dislocating joints or causing actual injury. In developing **transitional flow**, it is helpful to practice with as many different partners as possible so as to develop sensitivity to the wide range of reactions one might encounter given the different physical and psychological characteristics that make every attacker unique. In a time when physical distancing is recommended, one can engage in solo practice of **transitional flow** by *visualizing* the responses and positions of the opponent. In this way, it is possible to perform locks, strikes, throws, and chokes to air, much like a free-form kata. This may, in fact, have been the way in which kata were developed in the first place. Applying this concept to the origin of any given kata gives rise to a whole new realm of possible interpretations...

—Charles M. Terry, M.D., 5th Dan

o **Small Circle Practice Pointer:** At the more senior black belt ranks, students are expected to begin to chart their own courses, to make their own discoveries, and to share the fruits of their labors with the wider martial community.

XXIII. SELECTED TECHNIQUES:
Putting It All Together

Having reached 'the end of the beginning' so to speak, this is perhaps a good place to pause and cast a look backward over the ground we have covered:

o We have met the Founder and tracked the evolution of his art, from the hands of his own Master, to the Act of Succession and beyond.

o We have revisited the Ten Principles and added six new ones, eight precepts, and countless practice pointers to that arsenal.

o We have been introduced to the Technical Director of the art's stick-fighting component, and the drills he considers fundamental.

o We have discussed healing aspects of the art with the Founder's wife.

o We have explored pressure points, weapons, free-fighting and judo with several masters of the art.

o We have examined each category of technique (neck restraints, finger locks, wrist locks, arm & shoulder locks, groundwork, and throws) with various senior practitioners.

o And we have seen the integration of this art with several others through the eyes of one of the medical professionals who counts himself among the faithful.

Now is the time, then, to witness—and study—the way in which this all comes together when performed at the highest levels of practice...

Combination #1: Elbow block—Hammer lock—Control

1. Tori uses his elbow to guard and block/damage attacking fist

2. Tori's left hand (LH) slaps down on TW-6, 7 & 8

3. Tori drops his weight; RH grabs HT-2/LH slices into LI-12 & 13

4. Tori pivots and employs two-way action to lever uke's arm into lock positon [Tori's RH will finish by controlling uke's R shoulder/clavicle (not visible)]

○ **Small Circle Practice Pointer:** Tori's wrist to uke's elbow and vice versa.

Combination #2: Split—Strike—Wrist lock—Knee arm bar

1. Tori splits uke's guard: LH→ TW-6, 7 & 8/RH→ P-6

2. Tori's LH slides down to base of thumb for lock/RH→ ST-5

3. Tori's RH assists LH to perform 2H basic wrist lock

4. Tori finishes with squeezing knee arm bar with wrist lock

○ **Small Circle Practice Pointer:** Tori drops body weight to amplify effect.

Combination #3: Cover—Trap—Arm bar—Reverse wrist lock

1. Tori parries uke's R strike (w/LH) and checks LH (w/RH)

2. Tori's LH passes uke's fist into his R elbow to trap/lock and then pivots clockwise (pulling) to off balance and forestall LH strike

3. Tori's pivot not only takes uke's balance but also applies arm bar

4. Tori transitions to reverse wrist lock, L elbow→TW-11/12

Combination #4: Wrist Lock—Finger Lock—Arm Bar—Finger Lock

1. Tori adopts defensive stance; uke attacks by grabbing both forearms

This combination of techniques illustrates particularly well the way in which a smaller practitioner can employ body mechanics to overcome an objectively larger, stronger opponent. Uke's left wrist grab, for example, is no match for tori's right elbow, especially when assisted by her LH and augmented by dropping her body weight into the technique.

2. Tori drops her elbow over uke's forearm to apply bent elbow wrist lock

3. Tori transitions from wrist lock to finger lock to arm bar (R forearm vices HT-2)

Note: By locking the fingers of uke's LH and then using this lock as an anchor point to establish a compound elbow lock [above], tori dramatically increases the impact of this control. Likewise, by employing twin finger locks [below], tori effectively doubles the impact of the technique on uke.

4. Uke grabs with other hand and tori intercepts and applies *double* finger locks!

Combination #5: Arm trap—Knee arm bar with wrist/finger lock

1. Tori adopts defensive stance; uke strikes RH; tori parries LH and feeds to R elbow

2. Tori reinforces trap w/LH (on LU-5) and pivots L/drops weight to throw; then transitions to knee arm bar with finger/wrist lock.

Notes:_____

_____

_____

_____

Combination #6: Trapped arm shoulder throw—Finishing technique

1. Uke strikes RH; nage parries up/out LH; uke strikes LH; nage parries across RH

2. Nage's LH slides down to wrist (HT-6, P-6, LU-8)/RH controls forearm (LI-10)

3. Nage passes uke's LH into his own R armpit and locks by grabbing uke's R sleeve

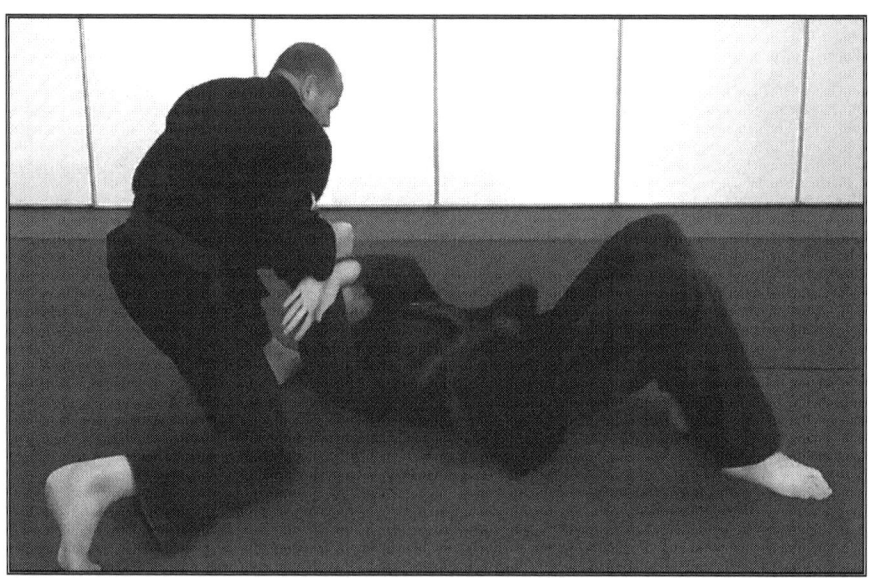

4. Nage pivots counterclockwise, throws over hip, and drops to follow up with strike

1. Uke pushes LH; tori parries down RH on back of uke's LH hand, grabbing fingers

2. Tori controls elbow (LH) and RH passes uke's LH under his arm to hammer lock

○ **Small Circle Practice Pointer:** This is an example of a compound lock.

Notes:_____

_____

_____

Combination #8: Parry trap (RH)—Finger lock—Arm bar

1. Uke pushes RH; tori parries down RH on back of uke's RH hand, grabbing fingers

2. Tori's L forearm and RH pass locked wrist up and out to elbow cradle armbar.

Notes:_____

XXIV. FUTURE OF THE ART:
What's Next?

The First Century: This book was published on what would have been Professor Wally Jay's one hundred and third birthday (June 15, 2020).

The Second Generation Headmaster: Born to Wally and Bernice Jay in 1955, Leon Jay is the Inheritor and current Headmaster of Small Circle Jujitsu. As a child, Professor Leon was exposed to the martial arts not only at the hands of his father, but also those of many other masters, including Bruce Lee, who frequented the Jay household. When asked to describe what it was like to have unfettered access to such training as a child, Professor Leon will often respond with a wry, "Yeah, it was *greeeaaat*," while absently massaging a half-remembered injury!

THE ACT OF SUCCESSION

When the then-not-yet Professor Leon decided that he did indeed want to be his father's successor it was not a done deal by any means! Professor Wally had little respect for nepotism. If you wanted to inherit even a family art, you'd better be worth it! He told Leon that he would certainly consider him, but that he should understand he wasn't the only candidate. He then told him he should come and train with me! What on earth he thought I was going to add to Leon's education, I have no idea; however, Leon said 'Fine,' and proceeded to travel around twenty miles each way twice a week to train in my apartment in Covent Garden for four and a half years! He never showed any resentment of the requirement set by his father, and Professor Wally would call me at least once each month to check on his progress. Plainly this was a test of ego and attitude and, needless to say, Leon passed with flying colors. If you've trained with him, you'll know that what I told his mother and father repeatedly in those days is true: He really is a worthy successor to his father.

—John Mellon, 7th Dan

○ **Set Syllabus:** One of Professor Leon's first initiatives was creating and adopting a standardized syllabus of techniques up to First Degree Black Belt. This innovation was especially important to students the world over who did not have a SCJ school in their region because it provided them with a roadmap for their studies, and helped in breaking a martial feast of intimidating proportions down into bite-sized pieces.

○ **Video Capture:** Going hand-in-hand with the syllabus was the creation of a DVD series committing each of the techniques required to achieve a particular rank to film. While such media are by no means a substitute for in-person training, they are of incalculable value to those who do not have regular access to SCJ instruction.

○ **Research:** Professor Leon continues to research the science underlying Small Circle Principles. For example, discussions with a medical doctor regarding the results of MRI scans established that brain activity increases significantly when tasks involving the fingers are being performed. This, in turn, may help explain the disproportionately powerful pain sensations that finger locks can produce.

○ **Integration:** Another salutary effect of creating a formal syllabus was the official integration of such adjunct arts as Modern Arnis and Pressure Point Fighting into the Small Circle style. Given the organic and ever-expanding nature of Small Circle Jujitsu, Professor Leon continues to study and integrate concepts from other arts such as Guro John Mellon's Munen Muso Ryu/Pindochin (Pan-Indo-Chinese Martial Arts).

○ **Tenth Dan:** Following the passing of the mantle of leadership in the Small Circle system, Professor Wally made it clear that he wished to confer the rank of Tenth Dan on his son during his own lifetime. Professor Leon, however, humbly declined at that time on the basis that there should be only one living tenth degree and that was, of course, his father. Many years later, after Professor Wally had joined the ranks of the past masters, Professors Tony Maynard and Dave Castoldi—who had been supporting the SCJ Midwest Camp for years—raised the issue again, based on both the passage of time and the direction in which the system was moving. Professor Leon describes the presentation of this uncommon rank by Professor Maynard and various other martial arts masters as, "a great honor."

○ **The Concepts Program:** Recognizing the value of cross-training and the desire of many experienced martial artists to augment their existing systems with his family's art, Professor Leon and one of his most senior instructors—John Mellon—created the Small Circle Concepts program.

THE SMALL CIRCLE CONCEPTS PROGRAM

In the early 1990s, Professor Wally, Professor Leon, and I regularly discussed the primary problem we were experiencing with the development and dissemination of Small Circle Jujitsu, i.e. that outside of each Professor's home dojo, there were very few places an aspiring student could access qualified instruction in the art. Despite Professor Wally having travelled for up to ten or eleven months of the year for more than twenty years, delivering hundreds of seminars all around the world, there were very few qualified instructors and dojos around. There were many thousands of martial artists who had been blown away by experiencing Small Circle Jujitsu at the hands of each Professor, but that hadn't translated into a large body of active students studying the full art.

I proposed that we create a program that delivered a cut-down, entry-level version of the art, which could be delivered in seminar format, giving the attendees the option of acquiring either a general grounding in the art, or specific technical skills, appropriate to their needs, that would allow them to 'plug a gap' in their technical arsenal, without the need to take on a whole new art to learn from scratch. Both Professors liked the idea, and Professor Leon and I set about constructing the program with Professor Wally's full blessing.

Because we wanted it to reflect the principle-based structure of the full syllabus art, we first tried teaching it in a format exploring each principle one at a time. Of course, this didn't work well; if you're familiar with the art and its Ten Principles, you will realize—as we should have done—that no single principle operates in isolation; one might be the dominant principle at work at any given time, but there are usually several others operating simultaneously in any movement consistent with the art.

So, we went back to the drawing board and altered the structure. We now have a program with multiple modules. There is the **Core Principles Module** (also known as Small Circle 101), which addresses all the basic mechanics utilizing a broad range of representative techniques and skill areas—if you just want to understand the basics of what makes this art unique and acquire enough understanding to increase the efficiency of your own background, this is the module for you. We have an **Entries Module**— you'll see that I've written about these elsewhere in this book. We have a **Body Throws Module**—if this is your weak point, or if you're a judoka or other specialist in this area, then this would suit your needs. We also have a **Weapons Module** and a **Finger-locking Module**, and we can even construct or tailor existing modules to meet the needs of your specific, existing skill-set.

The general idea is that you can dip in and out of the art to suit yourself, purely as supplementary training to your main art, if you wish, or you can acquire more comprehensive skills through a much smaller syllabus than the whole art. When we launched the first version of the program, we encountered a problem that we really didn't see coming: A host would attract stylists from many arts, from all around the UK, and some further afield, but when they hosted the subsequent sessions, some of the original attendees couldn't make it, and other new students wanted to attend. So then we had people missing new material, and others starting afresh, among those who had already acquired some basics, and it became impossible to manage.

To address this, the current structure is that all modules are certificated; you simply take modules in any order that address your need or interest at the time—and the certification simply documents that you have completed the training. Once you have completed the various modules, should you wish to take it further, you can enter **Instructor Training** to qualify to three separate levels: **Apprentice**, **Associate**, and **Full Instructor**.

Instructor certification is specifically for the Small Circle Concepts Program and would allow you to offer the art in that format to add to your existing school's programs. As the Instructor Modules are necessarily more intense, groups are much smaller, with much higher-level individual coaching (from either Professor Leon or myself). We therefore recommend this phase of training should be entered into with a 'training buddy'—it is easier to maintain one's commitment to the training between modules with a training partner, and as everyone is an individual, you will generally find that you and your 'buddy' will have different strengths and weaknesses both as practitioners and teachers, and co-teaching becomes a really useful learning device to develop further.

—John Mellon, 7th Dan

o **Pohai:** Professor Leon's administration of the Small Circle system has been informed not only by lessons learned at the hands of his father, but also by concepts from a variety of other systems in which he is *dan*-ranked, including Pressure Point Fighting, Judo, and Tae Kwon Do. Senior leadership of the Small Circle system is comprised of a number of experienced practitioners in various corners of the world, freely exchanging concepts, ideas, and students. This approach is entirely consistent with the Polynesian concept of *Pohai*—a Circle of Friends[4]—which has always informed the Jay family's approach to the martial arts.

[4.] Those who have tested for *dan* rank in SCJ are well acquainted with the alternative, and somewhat more sinister, meaning of the term: "A circle of friends…"

○ **Hombu:** In 1990, Professor Leon and his wife moved to Surrey, England, where he manages three different schools as well as overseeing the system as a whole. In addition, he frequently travels to various destinations to teach seminars and spend time with SCJ practitioners the world over. Professor Leon has been featured in a wide variety of martial arts magazines, including the April/May 2016 issue of *Black Belt* magazine, and has been inducted into the *Martial Arts Illustrated, Combat Magazine,* International Aiki Budo, and Modern Arnis Black Belt Halls of Fame.

○ **Schools and Seminars:** Small Circle schools continue to flourish in Atlanta, Arizona, California, Florida, Indiana, Maryland, Massachusetts, New Hampshire, New Jersey, New York, Nevada, North Carolina, Pennsylvania and Texas, as well as in several locations in England and France.

○ **The *Next* Generation:** Professor Leon's children—Liam and Grace—actively train in Small Circle Jujitsu…

XXV. WORDS OF THE FOUNDER:
The Final Lesson

◇ DON JACOB ◇

Professor Wally Jay was my best friend.

I first met him at the World Jujitsu Championships in Canada in the 1970s. My team and I—all black people from a third world country—arrived at the event and were 'housed' in a dojo basement instead of a hotel like the other competitors. Professor Jay knew that there was a team from Trinidad and Tobago in attendance, and when he couldn't find us, he came looking and found us training (in part to stay warm) in a freezing basement. After watching us practice for a while, he returned to the event venue and told the organizer, **"Those guys you put up in the basement are going to win this whole tournament!"** And it turned out, he was right! I knew right then that we would be friends for life!

After that first meeting, we traveled to many events together and he became like a father to me (I was raised primarily by my Grandmother) and many of my students. He used to joke, ***"That's my black son who looks more like his mother!"*** He was a deadly warrior but at the same time he also had a lethal sense of humor! He used humor to help people learn; to relax his students.

Once when he came to visit me in the islands, I organized a boat trip for him. At first he didn't want to wade out to the boat, so I carried him on my shoulders—the water was up to my chin—and he was holding on tightly all the way there! Then, when the trip was over, the same thing happened again! Afterwards, he confessed to me, ***"I cannot swim!"*** I told him, "Neither can I!"

Over the years, I also became close with Bernice Jay—she is an amazing woman—a wonderful wife, a fantastic mother, a powerful martial artist; a true queen (by the way, I chose the color purple to represent my system because it is spiritually associated with royalty in my culture). Bernice Jay was fiercely loyal and fiercely protective of Professor Jay throughout their marriage. I once tried to help Professor Jay with something while visiting their house and she said to me, "Don't make me put you over my knee— that's my job!"

Professor Jay's teachings had a profound effect on my martial arts training and he took me with him to teach seminars in many different countries. He also helped me to learn how to run a business. At one point he told me, ***"Stop collecting receipts."*** By this, he meant that I should try to buy the property where I was teaching rather than renting it from someone else. I now have schools all over the World, thanks to him.

Professor Jay was the ideal martial arts master. One of the most striking things about him was that even though he was tremendously powerful on the mat, he never threw his weight around. He proved his strength through action and always conducted himself as a gentleman through word and deed. He was never unnecessarily combative. If someone tried to challenge him, I would try to step in to protect him (even though he certainly didn't need it), but he would just use his sense of humor to deflect any aggression. He was also so relaxed because he had complete confidence in his abilities. When compelled to talk about the strength of his techniques, he would always say, ***"I am not bragging; I'm just confessing!"*** At first he called his approach "Small Circle Theory," but after it was established, I told him, "It's Small Circle Fact!"

Professor Jay's whole approach to life and the arts was that everyone had certain things that worked for them and certain things that didn't. He would say, *"You do your thing and I'll do mine. And if, by chance, we have anything in common, then we can co-exist, but if not, you go your way, and I'll go mine."* It was the ultimate "live and let live" philosophy. He was never argumentative or combative with people. He touched many different hearts in different ways...

One of the highest compliments I ever received from Professor Jay was when he told me, *"Your system is the most complete I have seen,"* with locks, throws, strikes, chokes, sparring, weapons, philosophy, and so on. We both agreed that the well-rounded martial artist should study all aspects of the arts. This includes the mental and spiritual aspects as well as the physical ones.

In fact, when he said, *"Pain makes believers,"* I think he was referring to more than physical pain; more than just twisting fingers and locking wrists. I think he also meant that we learn important lessons from mental pain, from emotional pain, from spiritual pain. Smart people can make mental errors; kind people can say thoughtless things; good people can have moral lapses. But the resulting anguish teaches them not to make the same mistake again. If you do not listen; do not feel; do not pay attention to people's intentions, then you will feel the negative effects in your life. I believe this was the deep truth of what Professor Jay was teaching. He was operating on a higher frequency...

I am so happy to be part of this special project. The fact that this happened shows that even from beyond this world, Professor Jay continues to bring like-minded people together...

—Don Jacob

○ ○ ○ ○ ○

When asked to provide some words of wisdom to endorse one of his student's books, Professor Wally Jay once said:

"For a true follower of the Way... the qualities of benevolence, courtesy and wisdom should accompany the skills of speed, power and grace."

The Professor's physical prowess was undeniable. He was known throughout the martial arts community for 'showing' rather than 'telling'. As he wrapped himself with his well-worn red belt and stepped onto the mat, he seemed to grow exponentially in size and strength. And for those who were honored to serve as his *uke,* it was a mixed blessing!

There is no doubt that the Professor was a powerful fighter. But as anyone who trained with him can attest, he was also a perfect gentleman. In fact, he adopted two Hawaiian terms that speak to the importance of developing proper character—*kokua* and *ohana*—as pillars of the martial art that he founded.

KOKUA & OHANA

Kokua roughly translates to providing selfless assistance to others.

Ohana conveys a sense of familial affection that can extend beyond bloodlines to embrace close friends and shared communities.

As noted at the outset, the character 'ju' in the word 'jujitsu' can be translated as 'gentle;' hence, jujitsu—'the gentle way.'

Those who train in this art, however, know full well that 'gentle' doesn't mean 'weak' or 'easy.' Yielding to an oncoming attack so as to blend with its momentum allows Small Circle practitioners to launch the opponent through the air and drive him into the unforgiving ground. Suppleness facilitates escaping any grip as a precursor to mounting a powerful counter-attack. And softness of touch allows them to forestall—and punish—the adversary's every move.

An American President noted many years ago during his inauguration at the height of the Cold War: "civility is not a sign of weakness." The world has never suffered from a shortage of strong people who are all-too-happy to throw their weight around. What is lacks—and desperately needs—is more gentlemen and women of quiet strength. Those who are confident enough in their abilities that they don't feel the need to advertise. Those who know that just because they *can* do a thing doesn't mean that they *should.* Those who *show* rather than *say.* Professor Wally Jay was such a man. He is truly missed...

○ **Small Circle Practice Pointer:** *Kokua* and *ohana* are at the heart of the art.

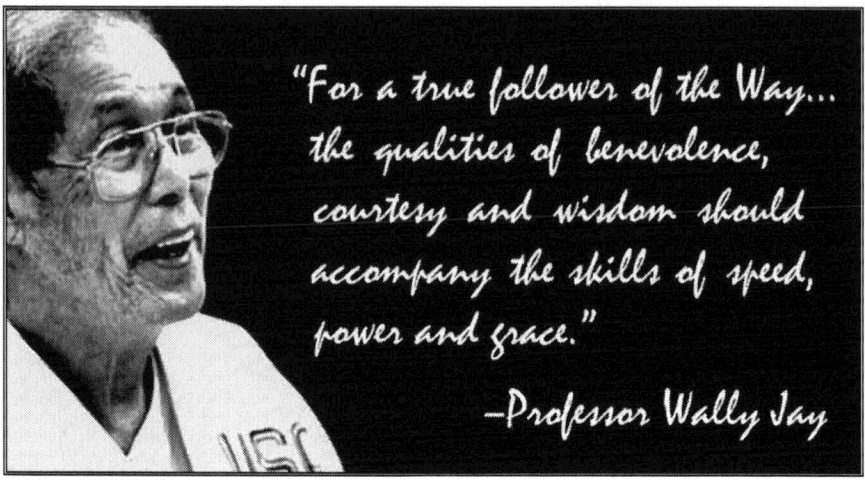

"For a true follower of the Way... the qualities of benevolence, courtesy and wisdom should accompany the skills of speed, power and grace."

—Professor Wally Jay

APPENDIX A—THE SCIENCE

FIRST PRINCIPLE:
Balance

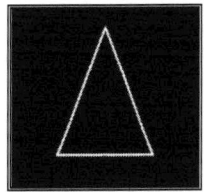

What is balance? In the realm of physics, it is simply a situation in which a body's center-of-gravity (CoG) is positioned over its base.[5]

---

[5]. Physicists may object that this somewhat simplified explanation fails to account for such variables as gravitational fluctuation, but this, and certain other conceptual liberties, have been taken in order to try to impart maximum of useful understanding with minimum extraneous verbiage; a kind of didactic conservation of energy.

As long is this condition is met, physical equilibrium is maintained. However, in order to appreciate this concept and its corollaries more fully, a slightly more in-depth examination of a few key concepts in the context of human biomechanics is required:

○ **Center-of-gravity (CoG)**: The center of gravity is a single, theoretical point—usually, but not always in the region of the *tanden*—where the entire weight of the body is equally balanced in every direction. Moving the CoG typically has the effect of moving the body as a whole.

○ **Base:** The base encompasses the entire area bracketed by the outer edges of the feet (or occasionally some other limbs on which the body may be resting). The number, position, and orientation of the supporting limbs can radically change the shape and efficacy of the base.

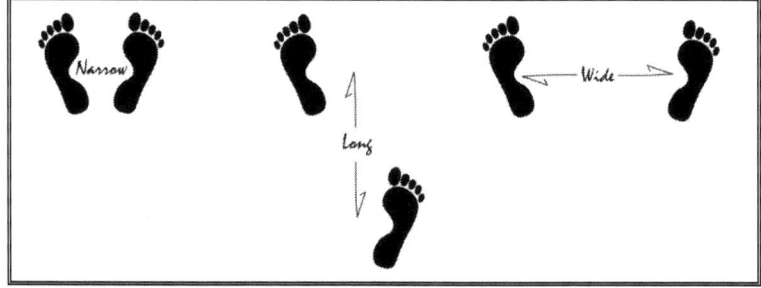

The interplay between these two concepts may be visualized as a triangle, the top of which is the CoG, and the bottom corners of which are the outer edges of the base (typically, the feet).

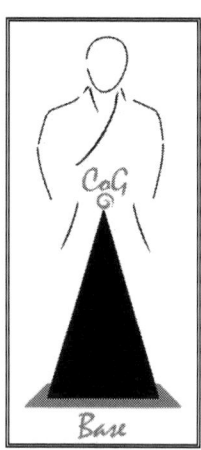

While the base has depth, as well as length and width, that depth is limited by the dimensions of the supporting limbs themselves. In other words, while the length and width of the base can be changed dramatically by repositioning the feet, its depth is somewhat more constrained, because no matter what stance the practitioner adopts, the dimension along the axis *between* the feet will always be limited by the size of the feet themselves.

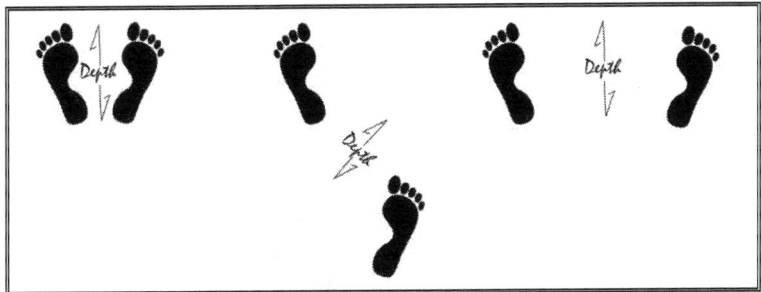

As a result, while a significant amount of motion can be absorbed along the length or width of a given stance, there is no orientation of the feet in which the CoG cannot be moved out of its *depth* by adjusting its position by just a few inches in the right direction. In other words, the triangle can usually be toppled quite easily by pushing its tip in a direction that is perpendicular to its plane.

While most throws involve doing significantly more than simply moving the opponent's CoG outside of his base, it is an important and helpful component of many techniques, in that it literally uses the opponent's weight—and the force of gravity—against him.

KUZUSHI, TSUKURI, KAKE

Known as *kuzushi* in Japanese, breaking the balance is the first of three essential stages in throwing. The second—*tsukuri*—describes the critical process of entry in which *nage* positions his body in the proper throwing position by fitting it to *uke*'s broken posture. If these first two steps are performed properly, the third stage, *kake* (execution), is a breeze!

✝— *Uke:* The receiver of the technique (usually the attacker)

♡—*Tori/Nage:* The executor of the technique/throw (usually the defender)

○ **Small Circle Precept—Sapping Energy:** In addition to the critical importance of breaking balance in throwing, Professor Wally often taught that simply keeping your opponent off balance throughout an engagement, even without throwing him, will sap his energy while conserving yours. Maintaining balance requires the delicate interplay of the visual, vestibular, proprioceptual, skeletal, and musculatory systems, and clinical studies have shown that the mere act of maintaining a balanced standing position can require a <u>third</u> more energy than sitting.

○ **Black Boxes:** While all techniques described in this work are potentially harmful, and are subject to the general disclaimer provided at the outset, a black box is used in these appendices to indicate those which are particularly dangerous.

○ **Small Circle Practice Pointer:** A blow to ear, which can effectively disrupt the function of the delicate vestibular system, thereby impairing the opponent's ability to maintain balance, can cause loss of hearing or other types of permanent damage, and should only be used in earnest in life-or-death situations.

SMALL CIRCLE EXERCISE—THE LEANING TOWER

In order to isolate and practice the **balance** component of the art, try leaning your partner forward, backward, sideways, and along the diagonals, just far enough to cause him to have to have to take a step in order to stop himself from falling. Performing this exercise with a partner who adopts a variety of different stances will help develop a feel for the point where the balance can be broken in almost any situation.

SECOND PRINCIPLE:
Mobility & Stability

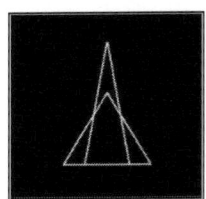

As discussed in the previous chapter, stability of balance is largely a function of the position of the center-of-gravity (CoG) relative to the base of a body. There are, in turn, five aspects of this relationship that can be altered to change the ultimate effect:

1. **Height of the CoG above the base:** The lower the height, the more stable the body. The greater the distance from the CoG to the base, the less it must be 'tipped' in order to fall outside the area of the base. For example, both of the figures below have been rotated -22°, but the 'plumb-line' of the CoG of the one on the left remains within the area of the base.

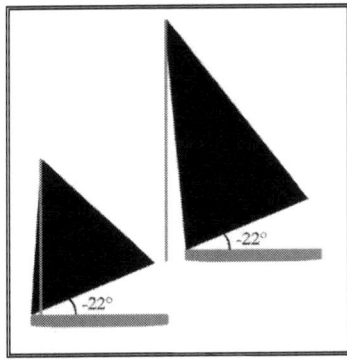

2. **Size (width of feet) of the base:** The greater the width of the stance, the more stable the body (the farther it must be 'tipped' in order to fall outside the area of the base). For example, both of the figures below have been rotated -20°, but the 'plumb-line' of the CoG of the one on the left remains within the area of the base.

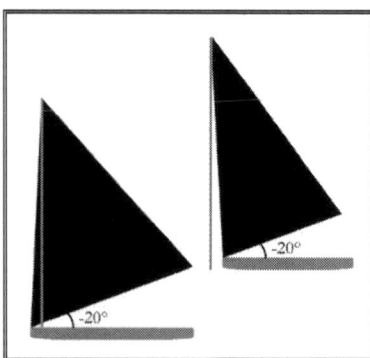

3. **Position (depth) of the CoG within the base:** The closer to the middle of the base, the more stable the body. If the CoG falls in the middle of the 'footprint' of the base, then it can be moved in any direction for a certain distance, like a sumo wrestler, without falling outside the permissible perimeter. For example, for the figure on the left (below), the CoG must be shifted half the width of the base in one direction or another in order to fall outside it, whereas for the figure on the right, the CoG is already next to the rightmost edge;

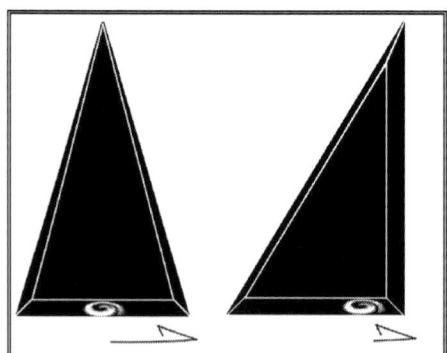

4. **Weight/density distribution:** The heavier and/or denser toward the base, the more stable the body. While there is very little the practitioner can do to change his density (or that of his opponent) on the spur of the moment, it is important to keep in mind that top-heavy objects/people are easier to topple.

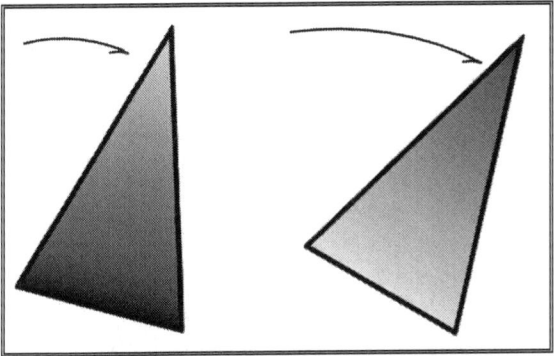

5. **The friction (gripping power) of the base:** The greater the friction between the base and the surface on which it stands, the more stable the body. While not directly related to the relative position of the CoG, the gripping power of the base also a key factor in establishing a stable posture. When barefooted, the mat or other type of surface can be gripped with the toes. While the wearing of shoes may impede this option, it is wise to keep in mind both the type of footwear and the nature of the ground at all times, not just in the training hall.

o **Small Circle Precept—Balls of the Feet:** Professor Wally taught students to maintain a low CoG when throwing or striking with power, but to allow it to rise when moving or transitioning. One way to do this is to move on the balls of the feet and ensure that the knees are over the toes (as opposed to the heels) when pivoting.

o **Small Circle Precept—The Bigger They Are...:** The greater the distance between the CoG and the base, the more unstable the object. This means, broadly speaking, that taller people are easier to topple. In fact, combining the five factors discussed in this chapter, a tall, skinny, top-heavy person wearing smooth-soled shoes and leaning to one side is a prime candidate to be thrown, ideally by a short, stout, bottom-heavy, barefooted individual in a balanced stance.

SMALL CIRCLE EXERCISE—THE DESCENDING ELEVATOR

Professor Wally taught his students the concept of lowering the CoG both physically and *mentally*. In addition to the physiological factors described above, simply by *imagining* the body traveling downwards in an elevator, the practitioner can increase his **stability** significantly, making it much harder for his partner (or opponent) to lift or move him. By developing and maintaining awareness of the existence and importance of each person's CoG, the SCJ practitioner can gain a decisive tactical advantage in any engagement.

THIRD PRINCIPLE:
Avoid Head-on Collision of Forces

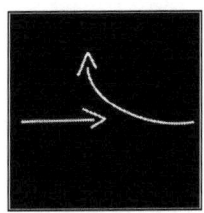

Newton's Second Law of Motion states that the sum of the forces (F) of an object is equal to the mass of that object (m) multiplied by the acceleration (a) of the object, or, rendered mathematically: F=m x a. In order to appreciate how this formula applies to human biomechanics, it is important to review a few fundamental ideas:

○ **Mass (m):** In the martial context, mass is generally a constant. The mass of the average human fist, for example, is usually a little over half a percent of total body mass. And while a punch involves more than just the hand, the comparative value of this principle remains the same regardless of how much of the body's mass is brought to bear by a given technique.

○ **Acceleration (a):** In this equation, a̲cceleration also includes d̲eceleration (which, in mathematical terms, is simply negative acceleration). This is an important consideration because the act of blocking or deflecting an attack will typically cause partial or total deceleration in the velocity of the striking limb. In order to calculate (negative) acceleration, the change in velocity (Δv) is divided by the amount of time it takes (Δt) to execute the technique. In this way, the basic formula F= m x a can be expanded to: F=m x ($\Delta v / \Delta t$).

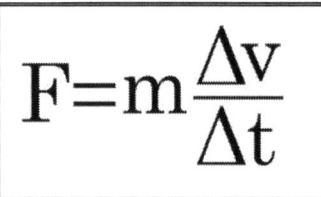

$$F = m\frac{\Delta v}{\Delta t}$$

In order to appreciate the power of this principle in play, consider the difference between stopping a hook punch with a hard block, and simply deflecting it:

Example A—Hard Block: Assuming that the mass of the attacker's fist (m) is **a pound-and-a-half**; the velocity of the attacker's hook punch (v) is **thirty** miles per hour; and the time it takes (Δt) to bring the punch to a full stop (Δv) using a hard block is **a tenth of a second**; then the resulting force on the defender's blocking arm would be **91.2 newtons**.

Example B—Deflection: The mass (m) of the opponent's fist does not change, but deflecting the hook punch does have an effect on velocity (v) and time (t). Rather than bringing the strike to a complete halt, a deflection simply redirects its trajectory, perhaps only slowing it to **fifteen** miles per hour (Δv). In addition, a deflection tends to make contact with the attacking limb over a slightly longer period of time; here, let's say **two tenths of a second**. By doubling the time (Δt) it takes to execute the technique, and halving the amount of deceleration (Δv) produced, the total force experienced would be reduced by three-quarters to **22.8 newtons**.

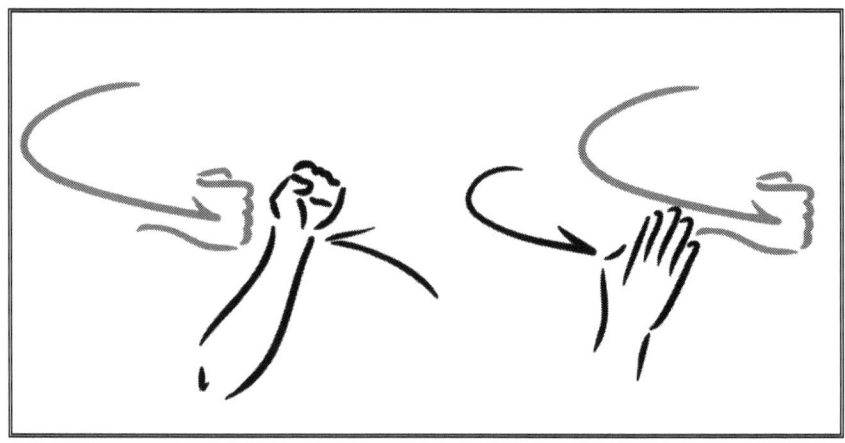

Vectors: Finally, the definition of F in the equation F=ma is the *vector sum* of the forces on an object. This means the total force is comprised of all amounts of force in any direction. When analyzing a **head-on collision**, there is only one vector to be considered, but when the contact is oblique, two or more vectors may be involved, with the force distributed among them. An appropriate martial arts analogy might be the breaking of a board: If struck at a perpendicular angle, all of the energy of the blow goes into breaking the board across its thinnest dimension (depth). If struck obliquely, however, some portion of the force of the blow will be distributed along one of the wider dimensions (length or width), making it less likely to break.

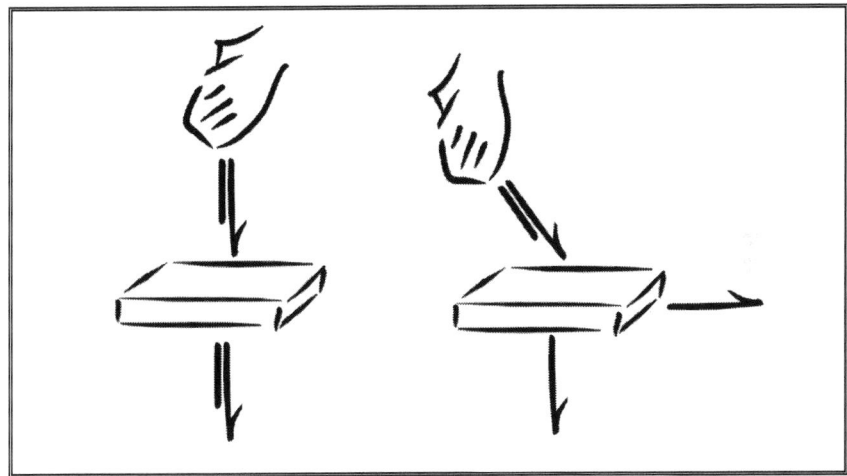

Accordingly, it is scientifically demonstrable that employing a technique (like a deflection) that **avoids head-on collision** can limit deceleration, increase time-in-contact, and divide vectors, all of which dramatically reduce the amount of force experienced *by both the attacker and the defender.*

○ **Small Circle Precept—Swing Away:** The Professor taught that unlike some other systems of martial arts, Small Circle Jujitsu teaches the practitioner to pivot away from—not toward—the opponent when blending, redirecting, or evading. In addition, he encouraged students to try stepping back or moving 45 or 90 degrees laterally to avoid a strike.

THE CHAMP—THE TALE OF THE TAPE

Watching film of Muhammad Ali—arguably the greatest boxer of all time—in slow motion shows him "milling on the retreat;" that is, backpedaling while counterpunching, absorbing the energy of the opponent's attack without sustaining any significant damage. Close study of the tape reveals that what look like a few, light jabs to the Champ's jaw in these situations are in fact very close misses. By retreating from the attack—by millimeters—Ali prevented forces from colliding head-on, while at the same time conserving energy and waging a subtle kind of psychological campaign to boot.

SMALL CIRCLE EXERCISE—THE SHOULDER DIP

One simple way to **avoid the head-on collision of forces** is to twist when struck ("turn when pushed"). In the case of a push, it is also a good way to create space in which to grasp the fingers. Partners can practice this by taking turns striking each other's shoulder's using a palm heel.

FOURTH PRINCIPLE:
Mental Resistance & Distraction

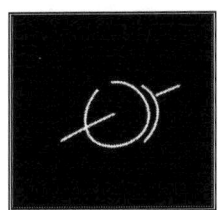

When examining the power of **mental resistance and distraction**, the scientific analysis moves from the realm of Newtonian physics to the dominions of clinical psychology and neurology. Multiple studies in these fields have validated the proposition that the mind can affect—and sometimes even control—the way in which the body experiences various stimuli, and in the martial realm, the stimulus of primary importance is *pain*.

In order to understand the way in which these scientific disciplines affect martial training it is helpful to define certain terms:

o **Pain Threshold:** The pain threshold is the point on a spectrum of stimuli where the subject begins to perceive discomfort. It might somewhat simplistically be thought of as the pain 'floor,' and it is generally fixed and objective.

o **Pain Tolerance:** Pain tolerance, by contrast, refers to the maximum level of discomfort that the subject can stand. Extending the architectural metaphor, this limit might glibly be referred to as the pain 'ceiling'. While clinical studies have revealed certain trends in this context—men appear to be able to withstand higher levels of discomfort than women, and tolerance seems to decrease with age—this threshold is somewhat subjective and can be consciously managed, at least to a degree.

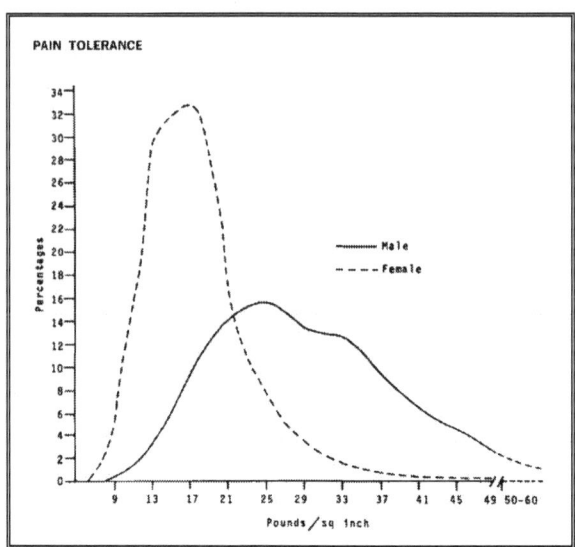

○ **Nociceptors:** Sensory nerve cells found, among other places, in the skin, which detect and respond to 'noxious stimuli,' such as pressure, heat, or chemicals.

○ **Central Nervous System (CNS):** The brain and the spinal cord, which have both ascending pathways for receiving sensory information, and descending pathways for transmitting appropriate responses.

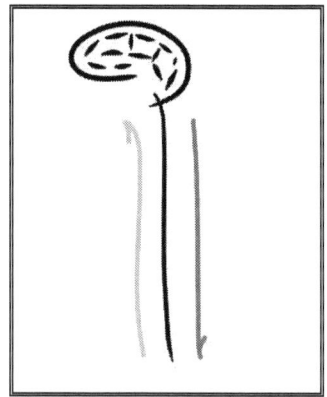

Clinical studies have repeatedly shown that the CNS is quite capable of reducing the sensitivity of the body's nociceptors (creating a condition known as "hypoalgesia") by, for example, releasing endogenous opioids like endorphins, enkephalins, and dynorphins.

ASSOCIATION AND DISASSOCIATION

There are two primary methods for increasing pain tolerance using the mind: association, and disassociation:

o **Association:** Focusing tightly on one particular aspect of the stimulus, or even the environment in which it is being perceived, so as to deemphasize the perception of pain. For example, concentrating on what information can be gathered from the degree of pain being experienced regarding the body's ability to continue to function under such circumstances, rather than simply allowing the emotional impact of the sensation to overwhelm the consciousness, can dramatically increase a subject's level of tolerance.

o **Dissociation:** Mentally disconnecting from the stimulus, and even the environment in which it is being perceived, so as to escape from the perception of pain. In many ways the opposite of association, this technique involves moving the consciousness away from the source of the discomfort, effectively blocking it from damaging the mind, and thereby reducing the (perceived) effect on the body.

SMALL CIRCLE EXERCISES—THE FLYWHEEL

Professor Wally often demonstrated the way in which students could resist significant amounts of pain, in effect raising their pain tolerance levels, using their **mental powers** of visualization.

o **The Flywheel:** For example, a bent elbow wristlock can be effectively resisted by imagining a flywheel spinning at high rate of speed in the opposite direction to that of the technique being applied.

o **The Unbendable Arm:** An armbar can be effectively resisted by visualizing a jet of water surging down the length of the arm and spraying from the fingertips.

o **The Unbreakable Ring:** And for simple demonstration purposes, the thumb and forefinger can be effectively fused into an unbreakable ring by picturing a circuit of water or electricity flowing between them continuously.

---

o **Countering the Counter:** As with any defense, however, there is a counter to these counters; a way to defeat the visualization techniques described above. A sharp kick or punch, a firm pinch, or even a loud *kiai*, can break the opponent's concentration and can serve to 'waken' him, making him susceptible once again to the power of the initial move. Extreme care must be taken, however, when practicing these counters and counter-counters, because the practitioner who is resisting in this manner will, by definition, be allowing himself to be taken outside of his familiar physical comfort zone. When pushing the envelope in this fashion, any sudden loss of concentration can cause serious damage. In addition, just as the execution of a sudden distracting technique can serve to break the opponent's concentration when he is resisting an attack (playing defense) it can also be used to forestall his attack (when he is on the offensive), or to gain a tactical advantage before either combatant has committed to a particular technique (neutral).

THE POWER OF KIAI

Dr. Charles Terry teaches that *kiai* serves several purposes:

1. It startles the opponent, breaking his concentration (offensive);

2. It may draw the attention of others who can assist (defensive);

3. It focusses the energy of the technique being used (offensive);

4. It prevents the wind from being knocked out of you (defensive).

FIFTH PRINCIPLE:
Focus Energy to the Smallest Point

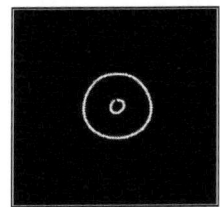

Returning to the by-now familiar ground of Newtonian physics, few concepts could be more axiomatic in this realm than: pressure (P) equals force (F) divided by area (A). Unlike some of the more arcane scientific principles discussed herein, this one makes immediate, intuitive sense: stepping on someone's foot with a high-heel will obviously inflict much more pain and damage than will the wide sole of a tennis shoe; a stiletto penetrates a body much more easily than a bread knife does; a target point burrows deeper into an archery butt than a broadhead; and a round-nosed bullet is likelier to shoot 'through-and-through' than is a wadcutter.

$$P = \frac{F}{A}$$

All of these observations are based on the idea that if the overall force behind a strike remains the same, the smaller the point-of-contact, the greater the pressure it will create.

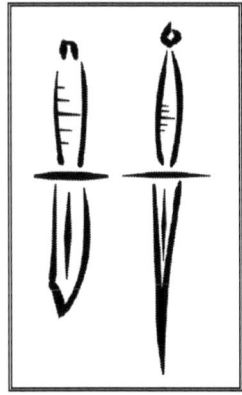

This principle is extremely useful in the martial context because it reminds the practitioner to make sure that contact is made by applying the sharpest available weapon to the smallest available target. Given that a fighter only has so much upper body strength, striking the collar bone with the knife-edge of the hand, for example, will cause much more damage that simply hitting in the region of the shoulder with a hammer-fist.[6] Locking the wrist will generally have a more powerful effect than attempting to control the entire arm, and locking a finger will typically cause more pain than simply controlling the wrist.

A FIGHT-ENDING TECHNIQUE

The finger lock is described by some as 'a fight-ender'. This is so because, once properly applied, there is almost nothing a victim can do to mount an effective defense. No matter how well-developed the body, a single finger will almost certainly be weak, at least comparatively speaking. Once 'activated,' the pain of a finger lock is usually enough to bring even the strongest fighters to their knees. And if held securely (with a proper **base** and the correct application of **two-way action**), there is really no viable escape route other than sacrificing the unfortunate digit altogether.

---

o **Small Circle Precept—Prying/Scooping Finger-lock Entry:** The idea of being able to catch an opponent's fist in mid-strike is more appropriate for the movie theatre than the dojo. The same is true for the thought of plucking a finger out of mid-air. But there are many ways to initiate a finger-lock that do not require superhuman abilities. One is to wait

---

6. Focused energy striking should not be confused with pressure point striking. While both will amplify the power of the technique, and they can be used together, they are conceptually different.

until the offending hand has come to a stop in the form of a grab, a push, or even a punch that has reached its destination. In such a resting state, there are several ways to isolate a handful of fingers.

○ **Small Circle Precept—Fortuitous Finger-lock Entry:** Another, surprisingly effective method is simply to wait until the natural give-and-take of sparring delivers a few fingers into your waiting palm. It is surprising how often this happens over the course of a short engagement, and those who are not trained in this sub-discipline are forced to throw away such golden opportunities to bring the opponent—quite literally—to his knees...

○ **Small Circle Practice Pointer:** Extreme care must be used when employing finger locks. The vast power differential between the shoulder, arm, and hand of the defender and the lone finger of the attacker means that it is quite easy to cause injury without meaning to. It is for this reason that Small Circle practitioners rarely practice these techniques on a single digit, preferring instead to grab two or more fingers at a time.

SMALL CIRCLE EXERCISE—THE TIP OF THE SPEAR

In **focusing to the smallest point**, it is important to choose both the weapon and the target carefully. For example, by modifying the shoulder dip exercise so that the push becomes a punch (and then an *ipponken*), and aiming for a pressure point like LU-1, the attacker can do a pretty good job of compensating for the defender's deflections.

SIXTH PRINCIPLE:
Energy Transfer

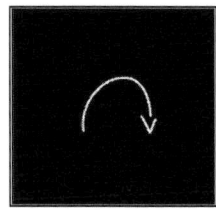

The latter half of the Twentieth Century, and the beginning of the Twenty-first, have witnessed an increasing number of Western scientific 'discoveries' whose basis—and sometimes entire genesis—lies in the province of Eastern antiquity.

The critical importance of the simultaneity of events in ancient Chinese cosmology, for example, finds support in cutting edge physics discoveries regarding quantum entanglement. The concept of a universe built upon binary code was fundamental to the theory of *yin* and *yang* millennia before the advent of the digital age. And Traditional Chinese Medicine (TCM), once considered a fringe practice at best by the Western medical community, has now become a common alternative mode of treatment in hospitals throughout the world.

It should come as no surprise, then, that Professor Wally's Sixth Principle—**energy transfer**—explained as *"chi* bleeding" in his first book, describes precisely the neurological concept of "secondary hyperalgesia."

○ **Small Circle Precept—Energy Transfer:** *"Energy transfer breaks your opponent's resistance more effectively than if you were to apply force to the area of focus immediately.... An example of energy transfer is the application of the reverse arm-bar, using knuckles against your opponent's triceps tendon. First, use a heavy palm by pressing your palm heavily against the opponent's forearm below his elbow. Then* **transfer the energy** *from there to the point of focus above the elbow, driving your knuckles directly into the tendon of the triceps."*—Professor Wally Jay, <u>Small Circle Jujitsu</u>.

○ **Neuroscientific Basis for Energy Transfer:** Several neurological studies, including one published in the *European Journal of Pain* in 2003,[7] clearly demonstrate that when pain (noxious stimuli) is applied to one part of the body, detected by specialized pain nerves at that location (nociceptors), and transmitted to the central nervous system (spinal cord and brain), the CNS can then send a responsive signal back down to the site of the noxious stimuli, making adjacent regions more sensitive.

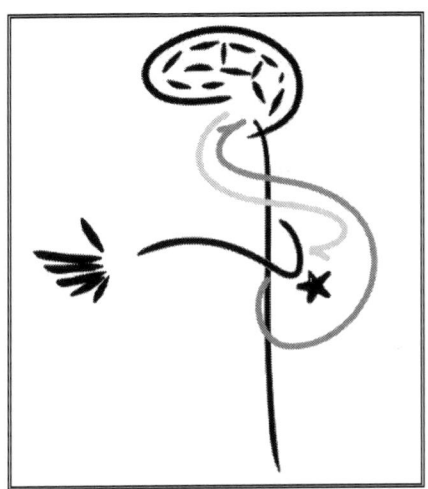

Various theories have been put forth regarding the precise purpose underlying this phenomenon, but the commonly accepted view is that the body's automatic response to the initial stimulus is to heighten its vigilance in the vicinity of the attack.

Clinical studies in the field of pain management have yielded many other findings in this context that echo martial arts teachings, particularly in the realm of pressure point fighting.

[7.] By Cervero, Laird, and Garcia-Nicas.

These include:

1. The phenomenon of remote—as opposed to adjacent—sensitization (in this regard, however, it should be noted that the Professor felt that the principle of **energy transfer** worked better over short distances);

2. Indications that the level of sensitization reaches a kind of 'terminal velocity' after three strikes; and

3. The possibility of consciously overriding the secondary **hyper**algesic effect in order to achieve the opposite result—**hypo**algesia (<u>see</u> **mental resistance and distraction**).

> ○ **Small Circle Practice Pointer:** Regardless of whether a terminal velocity of nerve sensitization truly exists, safeguards in the realm of energetic techniques include the exercise of extreme care with respect to: activating three or more pressure points in a cycle; striking corresponding pairs of points on both sides of the body at the same time; and targeting certain 'forbidden points,' especially in conjunction with existing physiological conditions.

SMALL CIRCLE EXERCISE—HEAVY PALM KNUCKLE ROLL

As Professor Wally wrote, one of the best ways to experience the power of **energy transfer** is to apply an arm bar using a heavy palm just below the elbow and then rolling the knuckles into the triceps tendon, but any technique in which force is applied first to one target and then another in close proximity can show the power of this principle at play.

SEVENTH PRINCIPLE:
Fulcrum, Lever & Base

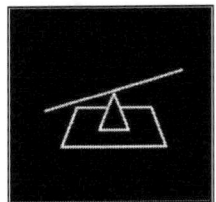

In the Third Century BC, the Greek physicist Archimedes is reputed to have said, "Give me a lever long enough, and fulcrum on which to place it, and I can move the world."

The power of the lever—which can be expressed using the equation $F_e = (F_l \times d_l)/d_e$, where F_e=effort force; F_l=load force; d_l=distance from load to fulcrum; and d_e=distance from effort force to fulcrum—was well understood even in ancient times.

$$F_e = \frac{F_l \times d_l}{d_e}$$

There are three main classes of lever:

Class 1: In first class lever systems, force (effort) is applied on one side of the pivot point (fulcrum) and resistance (load) is positioned on the other side. In other words, the *fulcrum* is in the middle of this three-part system. See-saws are first class levers (and scissors are double first class levers).

177

Class 2: In lever systems of the second class, effort is applied on one side of the load, and the fulcrum is positioned on the other side. Here, the *load* is in the middle. Wheelbarrows are second class levers (and nutcrackers are double second class levers).

Class 3: In lever systems of the third class, effort is applied in between the fulcrum and the load. In this case, *effort* is in the middle. Hammers are third class levers (and tweezers are double third class levers).

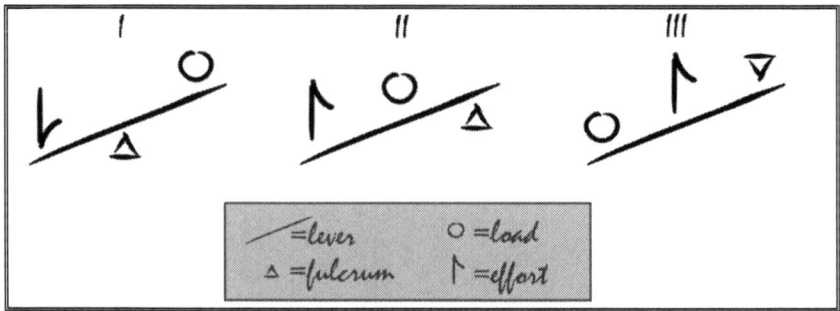

In considering Archimedes' principle, many people focus exclusively on the reference to "...a lever long enough..." glossing over the "...fulcrum on which to place it..." entirely. Omitting this seemingly collateral component, however, will render even the longest, strongest lever useless, because if there is no stable base from which to apply this tool, it cannot *work.

o **First Class Lever Techniques: Breaks**—When the goal is to break or threaten the integrity of the lever, it is important to immobilize the load—to fix it with a base. In this way, increased force will cause the lever to strain and break rather than simply moving the load. Arm bars and finger locks fit this model.

o **First Class Lever Techniques: Throws**—Sometimes the goal of applying leverage is to move uke with leverage. In such cases, the load is not fixed (but the fulcrum must still be stable). Many throws employ first class leverage. Applying force to uke's upper body, for example, causes it to pivot around nage's hips.

o **Second Class Lever Techniques: Neck Restraints**—Second class levers move a load that sits between the force and the fulcrum. Many neck restraints do this, as, for example, where tori applies force to his own hand so as to close the elbow joint (fulcrum) with uke's throat (the load) caught in between. When pressure is applied against uke's throat from both sides (by both the forearm and the biceps), a double lever of the second class is created.

○ **Third Class Lever Techniques: Strikes**—Third class levers move a load that sits at the far end of the fulcrum and the force. For instance, in executing a backfist, the forearm muscles (effort) move the forearm (lever) around the elbow (fulcrum) to apply force to the load (target).

○ **Small Circle Precept**—Especially when dealing with highly flexible partners, or those with high pain tolerance, creating a base against which leverage can be properly applied works wonders. Working with a solid base—whether it be the floor, a wall, or even some part of the practitioner's own body—takes much or all of the play out of leverage techniques, making them far more effective and secure.

> ○ **Small Circle Practice Pointer:** As noted above, leverage is frequently employed in neck restraint techniques (*shime waza*). Because of the delicate nature and position of the airway, blood vessels, and nerves in this part of the body, extreme caution should be used when practicing this kind of technique.

SMALL CIRCLE EXERCISE—FIRST ARM BAR

The power of the **fulcrum, lever, and base** can be seen in *many* SCJ techniques, but one that lays out the value and interplay of these components very clearly, and early on in the syllabus, is the arm bar with inside wrap (*kannuki gatame*).

EIGHTH PRINCIPLE:
Sticking, Control & Sensitivity

Human response times to tactile cues are significantly quicker than they are to visual stimuli. For example, a study presented at the International MultiConference of Engineers and Computer Scientists in Hong Kong in 2012 measured how quickly subjects could press a button when prompted using sight, sound, or touch. Tactile response times were a full third quicker than visual and auditory (with sound edging out sight by about 5%).

This is so, at least in part, because tactile stimuli are often processed by reflex, not conscious reaction. For a person to react to a visual stimulus requires the body's optic nerves to detect that stimulus, send this information all the way to the brain, and await a response. Tactile reflex arcs, by contrast, only have to send information as far as the spinal cord in order to receive further orders.

The simple "dollar drop" test serves to illustrate this principle. Holding a bill vertically by the top edge, invite your partner to position his hand in an open, pincer-like configuration on either side of the note, about halfway down, and catch it when you let it drop. Rarely will your partner be able to stop it from fluttering to the floor at your feet. Next, tap his hand with your free hand just as you release the dollar, and see how much easier it is to capture the falling money, even with his eyes closed...

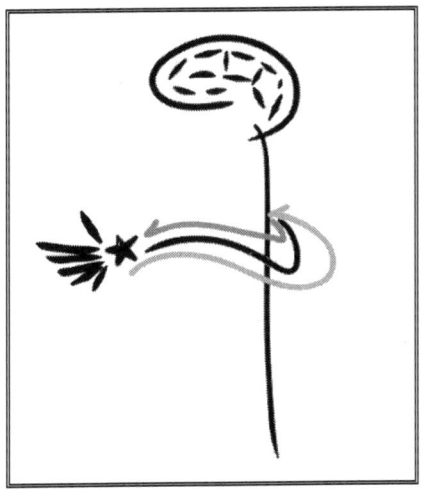

This shortcut can be seen at work in, for example, the reaction to touching a hot stove. The brain does not even need to receive the message for the body to respond by flinching. In fact, as a result of the so-called cross-extensor reflex component of this phenomenon, the subject will often move *both* hands away from the heat source—the one that was burned as well as the one that was nowhere near it.

SENSE	TYPICAL REACTION TIME
Visual	200-250 milliseconds
Tactile	130-170 milliseconds
Auditory	150-200 milliseconds

The Professor's Eighth Principle takes advantage of the clear edge that touch has over sight in terms of reaction time, allowing practitioners to *feel* the way that their opponents are responding to techniques in order to anticipate and forestall their evasions and counters more quickly. The Small Circle Jujitsu practitioner may only gain a few hundredths of a second of lead-time by augmenting visual information with tactile cues, but that is often all it takes to make the difference between victory and defeat.

o **Small Circle Precept**—The key to developing and employing the kind of sensitivity needed to sense the opponent's next move is to relax rather than tense up so as to be able to perceive the slightest stimuli. It is only in a quiet room that you can hear a pin drop.

o **Small Circle Precept**—The Eighth Principle can be employed both offensively (to detect the opponent's attempts to escape from a hold, for instance), or defensively (for example, by making light contact with the opponent's arm in order to detect the nature, timing, and direction of his next strike).

SMALL CIRCLE EXERCISE—STICKING HANDS (*CHI SAU*)

The **sensitivity and control** that physical contact allows can be both demonstrated and refined using the drill known as "sticking hands." By crossing forearms, and maintaining this linkage while executing techniques, practitioners learn to feel the opponent's posture, movements, and even intentions.

Appropriately enough, this practice can be augmented—either with or without a partner—by using a **small circle** of metal, known as a *chi sau* ring. Alone, the practitioner can develop a feel for moving inside and outside the opponent's defenses while maintaining continuous pressure through the use of this tool. In tandem, this device can be used like a link in the chain between two partners to hone the ability to sense and control the opponent's movements using only one or two points of contact.

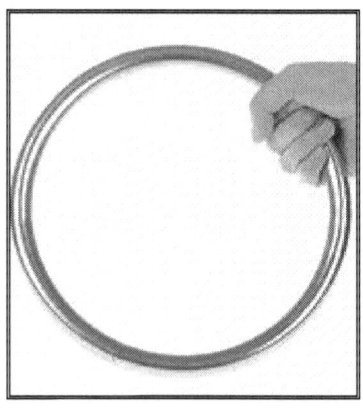

NINTH PRINCIPLE:
Rotational Momentum

It should come as no surprise that principles appearing toward the end of the list begin to incorporate aspects of some of those previously discussed. For example, from our discussion of the Eighth Principle (**sticking, control & sensitivity**) we know that it takes somewhere between one and two tenths of a second for the human body to respond to tactile stimuli, and longer when it comes to visual cues. From our study of the First Principle (**balance**), we know that one of the best ways to topple the opponent is to move his center-of-gravity outside the footprint of his base. Considering these two concepts alongside one another raises the question: "Can balance be broken before the adversary is even aware of the attack?"

Application of the Ninth Principle (**rotational momentum**) answers this question by saying: "Not only *can* this be done, but the opponent can even be lured into helping you to do it!" The scientific underpinning of this principle is based in large part on the biomechanical interplay between agonistic and antagonistic muscle pairs.

Take flexion (bending) of the elbow as an example. In performing this simple action, the biceps (the agonistic muscle in this scenario) tenses and contracts, but at the same time, the triceps (the antagonistic muscle here) relaxes and lengthens. In this state of enhanced relaxation, it actually takes longer for the triceps to reverse its function and tense up to extend the arm again than if no initial action had been undertaken in the first place. In other words, if the need to reverse direction arises, the antagonistic muscle is *already going the wrong way!*

○ **Small Circle Precept**—Crediting his own teacher—Henry Okazaki—with showing him the power of this principle, Professor Wally taught his students to begin creating *kuzushi* using the traditional two-handed, push-pull method of upper-body engagement and wait for the adversary to respond with opposing force before suddenly reversing the direction of the initial move in alignment with the adversary's resistance, effectively doubling the net effect. In this way, both the practitioner's and the opponent's agonistic muscles are working in the same direction, and the opponent's antagonistic musculature never has a chance.

○ **Small Circle Precept**—Over time, the term **"rotational momentum"** has been applied to certain other, powerful aspects of Small Circle Jujitsu. For example, rather than applying technique in a linear, or even uniformly circular, manner, experienced practitioners have come to realize that applying momentum in an ever-decreasing rotational spiral is devastatingly effective.

SMALL SPIRAL?

Professor Leon Jay has said that it is sometimes helpful to think of the "small circle" (*komaru*) referenced in the name of the art as a small spiral (*kokasen*).

Compare, for example, simply walking an opponent forward to a prone position using an arm-bar, with applying that same technique in a circular fashion, and finally with corkscrewing him into the mat.

o **Linear Arm-bar:** In the first example, the force of the arm-bar is working against the elbow (and the person to whom it is attached) in roughly a straight line. Accordingly, the opponent only has to react or resist in one direction.

o **Circular Arm-bar:** In its second incarnation, the force of the technique is continually rotating (centripetal force: $Fc=mv^2/r$), making it much harder for the opponent to assess, let alone repel.

o **Spiral Arm-bar:** The third version of this technique adds the power of the principle of conservation of angular momentum into the mix. Physicists tell us that angular momentum (L) equals mass (m) times velocity (v) times radius (r), and further, that angular momentum is conserved unless acted on by an external force.

If the distance from the practitioner's pivot point to the opponent's arm (the radius) is reduced by spiraling inward, and the rate of the practitioner's turn (angular momentum) remains the same, then the only thing that can increase is the speed of the opponent's rotation (velocity). Think of spinning a weight on the end of a long string and then gradually shortening it…

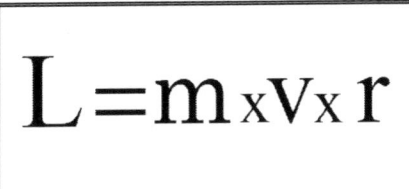

$$L = m \times V \times r$$

UKEMI

Finally, as **Dr. Charles Terry** explains it, *ukemi* (rolls) are used to transform the potential energy of a body being thrown from a height into kinetic energy, which is then safely dissipated through the **rotational momentum** of the rolling action.

SMALL CIRCLE EXERCISE—REVERSE DIRECTION

Rotational momentum—at least as Professor Wally used the term in his first book—refers to the technique of using the opponent's strength against him by pushing the opponent in one direction, causing him to resist, and then reversing the initial direction. Perhaps the simplest illustration of this principle at play would be attempting to circle to the inside of a wrist grab to execute *kote gaeshi* and, upon encountering resistance, reversing the circle to the outside to execute *kote mawashi* (or vice versa).

TENTH PRICIPLE:
Transitional Flow

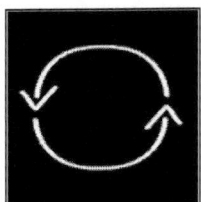

○ **Small Circle Precept**—Professor Wally taught his students that **transitional flow** was the most advanced aspect of Small Circle Jujitsu. The ability to progress from one technique to another in a seamless pattern is the hallmark of the art practiced at higher levels. In fact, much of the formal syllabus created by Professor Leon focusses on teaching and evaluating this critical ability.

THE DANCE OF PAIN

First generation students will recall fondly—and perhaps with a slight wince—being tossed around the dojo by Professor Wally in the grips of what he called, "the Dance of Pain!"

This Tenth Principle draws heavily on aspects of many of those which precede it. It is also guided by three components of its own:

A. Exert Continuous Pain During Transition:

○ The opponent is most likely to try to escape when the practitioner is changing from one technique to another. Multiple clinical studies confirm the common sense notions that: (i) subjects can be dissuaded from engaging in certain behaviors (like trying to escape) by negative consequences (in psychology, this is known as operant conditioning), and (ii) in addition, bodily pain has a detrimental effect on the mind's ability to function (in this case, plan and execute an escape).

B. Create Maximum Pain Without Dislocation:

○ How much pain should the practitioner seek to inflict? Legally, ethically, and tactically, the answer is enough to achieve the desired effect, but not so much as to cause damage. For example, if the goal is to deter the opponent from trying to escape, a wristlock can be applied powerfully enough to make him fear the pain of non-compliance without actually breaking bone or even straining ligaments. In fact, one of the most attractive aspects of this art is that an opponent can be writhing in pain one moment, and fully recovered the next.

○ Despite the practitioner's best efforts to guide the opponent toward the intended reaction, sometimes the desired behavior may not be immediately apparent. In these situations, the giving of verbal commands—an art in and of itself, commonly taught in the law enforcement community—can be of assistance. If the practitioner wants the opponent to stand up, he should accompany the technique with a verbal command to do so!

C. Mobility (Not Stability) During Transition:

○ As easy as it is to say, and as hard as it is to achieve, the key to maintaining **mobility** during transition is to *relax...*

○ Harking back to earlier principles, remember that **mobility** is facilitated by moving on the balls of the feet and maintaining a higher center-of-gravity.

UP, UP, UP!

In the same category as the Dance of Pain are fond memories of Professor Wally gleefully directing his various *uke*: "Up, up, up!"

The fusion of these three precepts, the preceding nine principles, and certain additional core concepts like **two-way action** and the **power of spiral motion**, gives rise to the expression of the art in its highest form. In the execution of every technique, the practitioner should assess the applicability and effectiveness of these teachings. **Transitional flow** is, in many ways, the "kata" of Small Circle Jujitsu.

SMALL CIRCLE EXERCISE—TRANSITIONAL FLOW

The best exercise for practicing **transitional flow** is transitional flow. For example, consider this possible defense against an open-handed push:

1. Pin the attacking hand (#8: Sticking, Control & Sensitivity).
   - The ring and little fingers are the most sensitive.
   - Physical linkage allows for reflexive reaction.
   - The resulting interplay is like 'leading' in dancing.

2. Turn obliquely (#3: Avoid Head-on Collision).
   - Blend with the forward momentum.
   - Move off the line of engagement.
   - Turning creates a 'pocket'.

3. Control wrist/elbow (#5: Focus to Smallest Point).
   - Grasp P-6 and HT-6 [fire] on the inside of the wrist.
   - Twist to bent-elbow wrist lock.
   - Drop elbow on LI-10 [metal] on outside of forearm.

4. Drop Stance (#2: Mobility & Stability).
   - Having moved off-line, drop down to create solid base.
   - Adds to effect of bent-elbow wristlock.

5. Backhand strike (#4: Distraction).
   - Striking GB-13-15 [wood] completes fire-metal-wood cycle.

6. Arm-bar (# 6: Energy Transfer).
   - Heavy palm to TW-10, then knuckles to TW-11.

7. Bend opponent forward (#7: Fulcrum, Lever & Base).
   - Knuckles are fulcrum, arm is lever, but there is no base!
   - Use body's maximum bend/hand on floor as base.
   - Use two-way action to enhance the technique.

8. Reverse to kote gaeshi (#9: Rotational Momentum).
   - If there is resistance to arm-bar, reverse to wrist throw.
   - Rotate in spiral to enhance the technique.
   - Use two-way action to enhance the technique.

9. Throw (#1: Balance).
   - By 'basing' the opponent, we have restored his balance.
   - Kote gaeshi moves his center-of-gravity outside this base.

10. Maintain Control Throughout (#10: Transitional Flow).
    - Keep constant pressure with judicious application of pain.

APPENDIX B—FOUNDATION TECHNIQUES

·◆· NECK RESTRAINTS ·◆·

One martial principle that has endured throughout the history of unarmed combat is: *"Where the head goes, the body will follow."* This is true even without the added 'incentive' of choking off the flow of blood or breath to ensure compliance. By encircling the neck just firmly enough to prevent escape, the head can be turned or otherwise manipulated in order to make the body go where the Small Circle practitioner wants it to, without risking lasting harm to the opponent.

ANCIENT KHMER BAS RELIEF SHOWING *HADAKA SHIME*

○ **Small Circle Foundation Technique:** *Hadaka Shime* (裸 絞 め) [literally: naked choke or restraint]—one of the most ancient fighting techniques that has survived into modern times—can be applied with sufficient force to capture and control the opponent's head without impeding his breathing or circulation (while still keeping these options available should the situation warrant escalation).

† Uke (the attacker) strikes with a right (R) punch;

○ *Entry:* Tori (the defender) parries and flanks uke, catching neck in R arm;

○ *Execution:* Tori's L hand reinforces R hand and closes R elbow to control.

○ **Practice Pointer:** Once the control is in effect, Tori tucks his forehead down to his own hands to protect his eyes and face from any counterattack.

○ **Practice Pointer:** Tori breaks uke's balance to the rear to thwart any counterattack.

○ **Variation:** There are many variations on this basic theme, including front naked restraint (fifth kyu); interlocking restraint (fourth kyu); lapel and sleeve restraints (third kyu); and the Hawaiian version (second kyu).

As of the time of this writing [6/2020], the following is a list of the neck restraint techniques from white to first degree black belt in the Small Circle Jujitsu system. As noted, however, this list is subject to change.

R-1 Front Naked Restraint—*Mae Hadaka Shime*—Fifth Kyu

R-2 Rear Naked Restraint—*Ushiro Hadaka Shime* —Fifth Kyu

R-3 Rear Interlocking Restraint—Hadaka Shime—Fourth Kyu

R-4 Finger Restraint—*Yubi Shime*—Fourth Kyu

R-5 Lapel Noose Restraint—*Eri Shime*—Third Kyu

R-6 Sleeve Restraint—*Sode Shime*—Third Kyu

R-7 Lapel Wing Restraint—*Kataha Shime*—Third Kyu

R-8 Windpipe Restraint—*Kubimoto Shime*—Second Kyu

R-9 Hawaiian Restraint—*Dansaiki Shime*—Second Kyu

R-10 Toe Restraint—*Boshi Shime*—First Kyu

R-11 Dragon Restraint—*Garyo Shime*—First Kyu

Notes:_____

_____

_____

_____

_____

_____

_____

·◇· FINGER LOCKS ·◇·

If *hadaka shime* is the 'granddaddy' of the neck restraints, then the index finger—*hitosashi yubi*—is the blueprint for the family of finger-locks.

> ○ **Small Circle Foundation Technique:** *Hitosashi Yubi* (人差し指) [literally: index finger]—Whichever finger (or fingers) are being locked, and whatever the orientation of the technique (inverted, reversed, compounded), the core concepts conveyed by this initial teaching will almost always apply.

1.   Two-way Action: In applying any finger lock, it is important to apply pressure in at least two places. In *hitoashi yubi*, for example, tori does not simply apply forward pressure to the end of the finger:

Pressure is <u>simultaneously</u> applied backward at the base of the knuckle:

2.   Create a Base: While not always necessary to make the technique work, creating a base will invariably make it more effective. In the version illustrated below, it is uke's own deformed posture that creates the base (allowing him no further flexibility to move in order to relieve the pressure);

3.   Small Spiral [New Principle]: Tori's application of force is not just circular; it is spiral. That is to say, the rotational force is applied to uke's finger in an ever-decreasing circle.

INDEX FINGER LOCK—*Hitosashi Yubi*—EIGHTH KYU

○ *Entry:* One way to make entry for this technique is for tori to twist sideways to create a 'pocket' in response to an open-handed push to the chest;

○ *Execution:* Once the index finger is grasped, the tip is rotated forward while the base is pulled back (two-way action).

○ **Application:** This technique can be used to move uke up-down, left-right, backward-forward (safer with two fingers) and amplified by creating a base.

○ **Variation (Thumb-to-Knuckle):** This technique can also be applied with a more distal grasp on the finger by adding outward pressure to help lock the digit into tori's grip.

As of the time of this writing [6/2020], the following is a list of the finger locks from white to first degree black belt in the Small Circle Jujitsu system. As noted, however, this list is subject to change.

F-1 Index Finger Lock—*Hitosashi Yubi*—Eighth Kyu

F-2 Thumb Compression Lock—*Oya Yubi*—Eighth Kyu

F-3 Inverted (Hand) Finger Lock—*Gyaku Te*—Seventh Kyu

F-4 Ring Finger Lock—*Naka Te*—Sixth Kyu

F-5 All Finger (Fist) Lock—*Seiken*—Sixth Kyu

F-6 Reverse Finger Lock—*Gyaku Yubi*—Fifth Kyu

F-7 Double Inverted Finger Lock—*Ryote Gyakute*—Fourth Kyu

F-8 C-Lock—*Hangetsu*—Fourth Kyu

F-9 Third Finger Lock—*Kusuri Yubi*—Second Kyu

F-10 Interlocking Finger Lock—*Amido Yubi*—Second Kyu

Notes:_____

_____

_____

_____

_____

_____

_____

_____

·◊· GRAPPLING ·◊·

Just as *hadaka shime* is the 'granddaddy' of the neck restraints, and *hitosashi yubi* is the blueprint for the family of finger-locks, the mount & guard (*shiho gatame* and *do osae*) illustrate the core principle of grappling: Positioning your entire body in the most advantageous position relative to the opponent.

○ **Small Circle Foundation Technique:** ***Shiho Gatame/Do Osae*** (四方固/胴押) [literally: four directional control/torso press]—Notice how the mount and the guard are actually the same with the opponent's positions simply reversed. In the mount, tori (black) is on top and uke (grey) is on the ground. In the guard, uke is on top, and tori is on the ground. In both cases, however, tori keeps uke at bay by locking his legs around uke's waist. In this way, tori can reach uke's head whereas uke cannot, despite the fact that their arms are the same length.

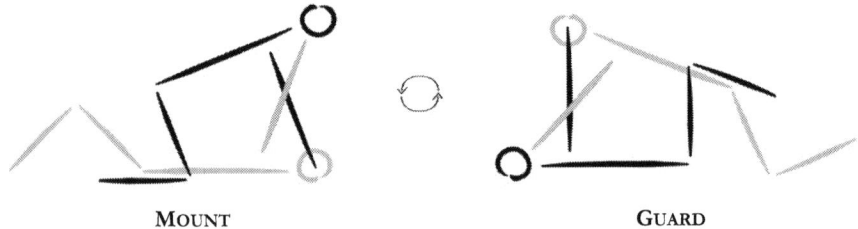

MOUNT   GUARD

1.   Body Position: In any ground engagement, victory will likely go to the combatant who first achieves superior positioning. For this reason, the Small Circle syllabus emphasizes the importance of transitioning properly from stand-up fighting to ground grappling, whether taking down the opponent, or being taken down by the opponent.

2.   Leg Control: The legs so vastly out-power the arms that it is important to bring these powerful limbs into play whenever possible. Here, by gripping uke's torso with the knees, tori makes escape virtually impossible.

3.   Arms on the Inside Track: In virtually any grappling situation, it is advantageous to control the inside track with your arms. As a threshold matter, the shortest distance between two points is a straight line, and in addition, simply occupying the midline can serve to deflect or diminish the power of the opponent's hand strikes.

○ *Entry:* Tori takes uke down and drops into a kneeling position sitting astride uke's upper body.

○ *Variation:* The Guard is simply an inverted mount (tori is on his back).

○ **Practice Pointer:** The mount pins uke down while providing tori with an advantageous position and angle for delivering follow-up techniques.

○ **Practice Pointer:** At Fifth Kyu, students are taught to perform a Japanese Armbar from the Mount.

Notes:_____

As of the time of this writing [6/2020], the following is a list of the grappling techniques from white to first degree black belt in the Small Circle Jujitsu system. As noted, however, this list is subject to change.

G-1 Scarf Hold—*Kesa Gatame*—Seventh Kyu

G-2 Shoulder Hold—*Kata Gatame*—Seventh Kyu

G-3 The Mount—*Shiho Gatame*—Sixth Kyu

G-4 The Guard—*Do Osae*—Sixth Kyu

G-5 Double Lapel Restraint—*Ryote Shime*—Fourth Kyu

G-6 Arm Bar-8: Cross-body—*Ude Garami*—Third Kyu

G-7 Figure Four Leg Lock—*Ashi Garami*—Third Kyu

G-8 Grapevine—*Tate Shiho Gatame*—Third Kyu

G-9 Arm Bar-8: Shin Kneeling—*Sune Ude Hishigi*—Second Kyu

G-10 Triangle Restraint—*Sankaku Shime*—Second Kyu

Notes:_____

_____

_____

_____

_____

_____

_____

_____

·◊· THROWS ·◊·

The majority of the throwing techniques in the initial stages of Small Circle practice revolve around one of two main tools: The **hip** and the **trip**. Of the wide variety of ways to throw uke using the hip, the **Major Hip Throw** is perhaps the first among equals, and there are many ways of reaping, stopping, or tripping the opponent, beginning with the **Major Outer Reap**.

> ○ **Small Circle Foundation Technique:** *O Goshi* (大腰) [literally: major hip]—Of the twenty-odd throws in the Small Circle syllabus from white to first degree black belt, eight of them involve rotating uke's mass around the hip or shoulder, or a similar kind of action. As a result, this is a critical skill to master early on.

    1.   Leverage: Given sufficient effort, most people can haul a mass that is close to their own body weight over their shoulder. But the art of the throw lies in positioning the fulcrum of the throw (here: the hip) so perfectly that minimal effort is needed to topple the opponent. This requires taking a stance that is low and deep enough to get *under* the opponent's center-of-gravity.

    2.   Augmentation: There are many ways to use the upper body (arms and hands) to augment the power of the lower body (hips and legs) in executing a throw. In addition to breaking uke's balance when gripping up, for example, Professor Leon will often press on a vulnerable point to 'encourage' uke to move in the right direction…

> ○ **Small Circle Foundation Technique:** *O Soto Gari* (大外刈) [literally: major outer reap]—Of the twenty-odd throws in the Small Circle syllabus from white to first degree black belt, nine of them involve disrupting uke's stance with a reaping, sweeping, tripping, or stopping action with the leg. As a result, this is a critical skill to master early on.

    1.   Timing: In any technique that involves removing one (or both) of uke's supporting legs, it is critical to time the move appropriately. If the target leg is firmly planted when the technique is attempted, it may be possible to break its grip on the ground through the application of superior force, but this lacks the grace and artistry of gently and easily sweeping it aside when it is in motion and therefore not grounded.

    2.   Amplification: In addition to ease of execution, if the target leg is removed at the precise moment that uke is attempting to place weight on it, the momentum of his unsupported fall can be used to amplify the technique.

HIP THROW—*O Goshi*—EIGHTH KYU

○ *Kuzushi:* Nage pulls **uke's R** sleeve and wraps own right arm around the hip; **[contact is given with reference to uke's position]**

○ *Tsukuri:* Nage enters closely (L135) and places R hip against uke's abdomen;

○ *Kake:* Nage uses his hip as a pivot to topple uke to **his** front/right quadrant. **[actions are described with reference to nage's position]**

o **Practice Pointer:** It is important to leave enough space when entering to break uke's balance by pulling him forward and slightly to his right.

o **Practice Pointer:** Nage's feet remain *inside* uke's stance during the throw.

o **Follow-on:** Nage retains hold of uke's R arm throughout the technique in order to follow up the throw seamlessly with a hand/arm technique.

Notes:_____

_____

○ *Kuzushi/Tsukuri:* Nage 'grips up': LH to uke's R sleeve, RH to uke's L lapel
Nage's LH pulls back/down/left; RH pushes forward/up/left;

○ *Kake:* Nage drives his R leg forward, then back, sweeping uke's R leg back.

○ **Practice Pointer:** Uke's balance should actually be broken to the back-right quadrant (*uke's* back-right quadrant) before nage even sweeps the leg.

○ **Practice Pointer:** Nage tucks his head on entry to avoid a counterstrike.

○ **Variation:** Can also be executed following inside line block from strike.

○ **Practice Pointer:** Can be amplified *dramatically* by striking in/down on LU-1/2 with RH using wrist twist, shoulder drop, hip turn, and gravity.

Notes:_____

_____

As of the time of this writing [6/2020], the following is a list of the throws from white to first degree black belt in the Small Circle Jujitsu system. As noted, however, this list is subject to change.

T-1 Major Outer Reap—*O Soto Gari*—Eighth Kyu

T-2 Hip Throw—*O Goshi*—Eighth Kyu

T-3 One Arm Shoulder Throw—*Ippon Seionage*—Seventh Kyu

T-4 Double Sleeve Throw—*Tai Otoshi*—Seventh Kyu

T-5 Drop Leg Shoulder Throw—*Seio Otoshi*—Seventh Kyu

T-6 Major Inner Reap—*O Uchi Gari*—Sixth Kyu

T-7 Hook Foot Sweep—*De Ashi Barai*—sixth Kyu

T-8 Minor Inner Reap—*Ko Uchi Gari*—Fifth Kyu

T-9 Minor Outer Reap—*Ko Soto Gari*—Fifth Kyu

T-10 Double Arm Lift Throw—*Tenchi Nage*—Fourth Kyu

T-11 Double Sleeve Throw—*Hiza Otoshi*—Fourth Kyu

T-12 Knee Locks—*Hiza Waza*—Fourth Kyu

T-13 Trapped Arm Shoulder Throw—*Seionage*—Third Kyu

T-14 Leg Stop—*Hiza Guruma*—Third Kyu

T-15 Headlock and Rear Drop—*Kubi Nage*—Second Kyu

T-16 Winding Throw—*Makikomi*—Second Kyu

T-17 Stomach Throw—*Tomoenage*—First Kyu

T-18 Flying Scissors—*Kani Basami*—First Kyu

T-19 Front Sacrifice Throw—*Mae Sutemi Nage*—First Kyu

T-20 Back Sacrifice Throw—*Ushiro Sutemi Nage*—First Kyu

Notes:_____

_____

_____

_____

·◊· Arm & Shoulder Locks ·◊·

As with the throws, the majority of the arm and shoulder locks in the initial stages of Small Circle practice revolve around one of two main actions: Moving either (and sometimes both) the elbow joint and/or the shoulder joint in ways that nature never intended.

○ **Small Circle Foundation Technique:** *Kannuki Gatame* (閂固め) [literally: gate control]—Of the fifteen-odd arm and shoulder locks in the Small Circle syllabus from white to first degree black belt, six of them involve applying pressure directly against the elbow joint. As a result, this is a critical skill to master early on.

---

1. Variations: There are myriad ways to attack the elbow. With *Kannuki Gatame,* this joint is isolated with both arms while keeping tori safely off to the side (*see* below). With *Gyaku Ude Hishigi,* it is combined with a wrist lock to drive uke to the ground. With *Hiji Gatame,* it is applied as part of an escape from a bear hug. With *Ashi Osae,* the pressure is applied using the knees…

2. Key Principles: As with so many other techniques, in order to maximize the effect of this attack, it is important to remember to employ **Two-way Action**, applying opposing pressure to the elbow and the arm, and to ensure that Uke remains off **Balance** throughout the application of the technique to minimize the chances of a counterstrike.

○ **Small Circle Foundation Technique:** *Ude Guruma* (腕車) [literally: arm wheel]—Of the fifteen-odd arm and shoulder locks in the Small Circle syllabus from white to first degree black belt, eight of them involve hyper-rotating the ball-and-socket joint of the shoulder. As a result, this is a critical skill to master early on.

---

1. Variations: There are myriad ways to attack the shoulder. With *Ude Guruma* (as well as *Ude Garami, Hiji Makikomi, and Gyaku Hiji Makikomi*) this joint is hyper-rotated backward. With *Gyaku Ude Garami,* it is hyper-rotated forward while keeping tori safely behind the opponent. And with *Gyaku Ude Hishigo Makikomi,* it is combined with an elbow attack.

2. Key Principles: As with so many other techniques, in order to maximize the effect of this attack, it is important to remember to **Create a Base** so that uke cannot relieve the pressure on the joint, and to employ **Sticking Control and Sensitivity** to detect and neutralize any escape attempt.

ARM BAR-1: INSIDE WRAP—*Kannuki Gatame*—SEVENTH KYU

† *Attack:* Uke strikes with a high straight punch (RH);

○ *Entry:* Tori RH parries L→R, catches wrist, snakes LH over/around elbow;

○ *Execution:* Tori levers trapped wrist forward over fulcrum of own L forearm.

○ **Practice Pointer:** Because tori parries from the *outside*, there is less danger of a counter-strike from uke's off-side hand.

○ **Practice Pointer:** Tori 'bases' his LH by grabbing his own gi, or bracing against his R forearm.

Notes:_____

_____

_____

Arm And Shoulder Lock—*Ude Guruma*—Seventh Kyu

† *Attack:* Uke strikes with a high hook punch (RH);

♡ *Entry:* Tori LH parries R→L, feeds RH outside elbow/behind wrist;

♡ *Execution:* Tori rotates RH forward to lock/throw.

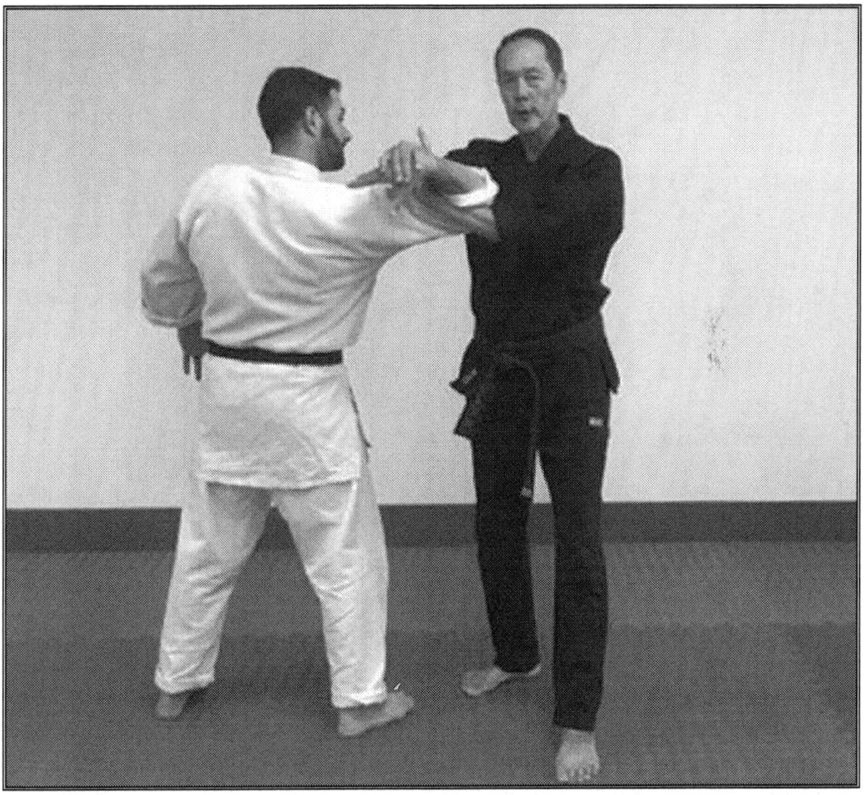

○ **Practice Pointer:** As with any move in which tori parries from the *inside*, it is especially important to check the offside hand so as to prevent a counter-strike while executing the technique. It is often advisable to throw in a distracting strike before transitioning to the lock/throw.

○ **Practice Pointer:** This technique can be concluded with a throw known as *shiho nage*—the four directional throw (because from this entry, nage can throw uke in almost any direction).

As of the time of this writing [6/2020], the following is a list of the arm and shoulder locks from white to first degree black belt in the Small Circle Jujitsu system. As noted, however, this list is subject to change.

A-1 Arm and Shoulder Lock—*Ude Guruma*—Seventh Kyu

A-2 Hammer Lock—*Gyaku Ude Garami*—Seventh Kyu

A-3 Arm Bar-1: Inside Wrap—*Kannuki Gatame*—Seventh Kyu

A-4 Arm Bar-2: Reverse—*Gyaku Ude Hishigi*—Seventh Kyu

A-5 Reverse Hammer Lock—*Kosa Gyaku Ude Garami*—Sixth Kyu

A-6 Winding Lock—*Hiji Makikomi*—Sixth Kyu

A-7 Arm Bar-3: Cross Reverse—*Kosa Gyaku Ude Hishigi*—Sixth Kyu

A-8 Arm Trap—*Hiji Otoshi*—Fifth Kyu

A-9 Snaking Lock—*Gyaku Hiji Makikomi*—Fifth Kyu

A-10 Figure Four Lock—*Ude Garami*—Fourth Kyu

A-11 Arm Bar-4: Figure Four—*Ude Hishigi Makikomi*—Third Kyu

A-12 Arm Bar-5: Reverse Figure Four— *Gyaku Ude Hishigi Makikomi*

A-13 Hand and Elbow Lock—*Hijite Osae*—Third Kyu

A-14 Arm Bar-6: Bear Hug—*Hiji Gatame*—Second Kyu

A-15 Arm Bar-7: Squeezing Knee—*Ashi Osae*—Second Kyu

Notes:_____

_____

_____

_____

·◇· WRIST LOCKS ·◇·

Whereas throws and arm locks tend to follow either of *two* patterns, the primary wrist locks fall into *four* main categories:

A.   Wrist bent down, turn in (counterclockwise)—As in Basic Wrist Lock.
B.   Wrist bent down, turn out (clockwise)—As in Reverse Wrist Lock;
C.   Wrist bent back, turn in (clockwise)—As in Vertical Wrist Lock;
D.   Wrist bent back, turn out (counterclockwise)—As in Hand/Elbow Lock;

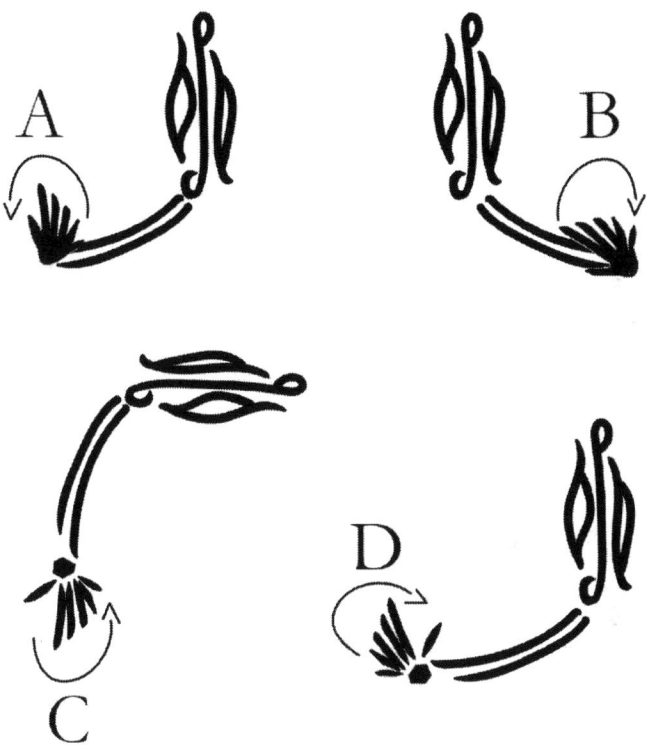

- **Small Circle Foundation Technique:** *Kote Gaeshi* (小手返し) [literally: wrist reversal].
- **Small Circle Foundation Technique:** *Kote Mawashi* (小手廻し) [literally: wrist revolution].
- **Small Circle Foundation Technique:** *Kote Hineri* (小手捻り) [literally: wrist twist].
- **Small Circle Foundation Technique:** *Hijite Osae* (肘手押) [literally: elbow-hand press].

BASIC WRIST LOCK—*Kote Gaeshi*—EIGHTH KYU

† Uke extends his right hand [RH], as with a shuto, punch, backhand strike;

○ Tori grasps back of uke's RH with RH, thumb between 4th & 5th knuckles;

○ Tori twists uke's RH counter-clockwise to take uke down to the ground.

○ **Practice Pointer:** Tori uses thumb to press into TW-3 (fire) on back of uke's hand and finger(s) to cut into LU-8 (metal) on uke's inner wrist.

○ **Practice Pointer:** Energy should be applied toward uke's centerline.

○ **Variation:** This technique can be applied same, cross, or two-handed.

Notes:_____

_____

_____

_____

† Uke extends his right hand [RH], as with a shuto, punch, backhand strike;

○ Tori grasps back of uke's RH with RH, thumb in web of uke's hand;

○ Tori twists uke's RH clockwise to take uke down to the ground.

○ As shown below, tori's LH can assist.

○ **Practice Pointer:** Tori uses thumb to press into LI-4 (metal) on web of uke's hand and little finger to cut into HT-6 (fire) on uke's inner wrist.

○ **Practice Pointer:** Energy should be applied toward uke's centerline.

○ **Variation:** This technique can be applied two-handed.

Notes:_____

VERTICAL WRIST LOCK—*Kote Hineri*—SEVENTH KYU

† Uke grabs tori's right wrist with his right hand;

♡ Tori circles grabbed wrist clockwise and grasps uke's RH with LH;

♡ Tori rotates uke's RH in an upward/clockwise spiral applying the lock.

○ **Practice Pointer:** Tori uses his thumb to press into LI-4 (metal) and his index finger to cut into HT-8 (fire) on uke's palm.

○ **Practice Pointer:** Upward pressure must be maintained for this to work.

○ **Variation:** This technique can be applied cross-handed or two-handed.

Notes:_____

_____

_____

HAND AND ELBOW LOCK—*Hijite Osae*—THIRD KYU

† *Attack:* Uke pushes against tori's chest (RH);

♡ *Entry:* Tori pins uke's RH to chest with LH and cups uke's elbow with RH;

♡ *Execution:* Tori pulls elbow toward own chest and leans forward to lock.

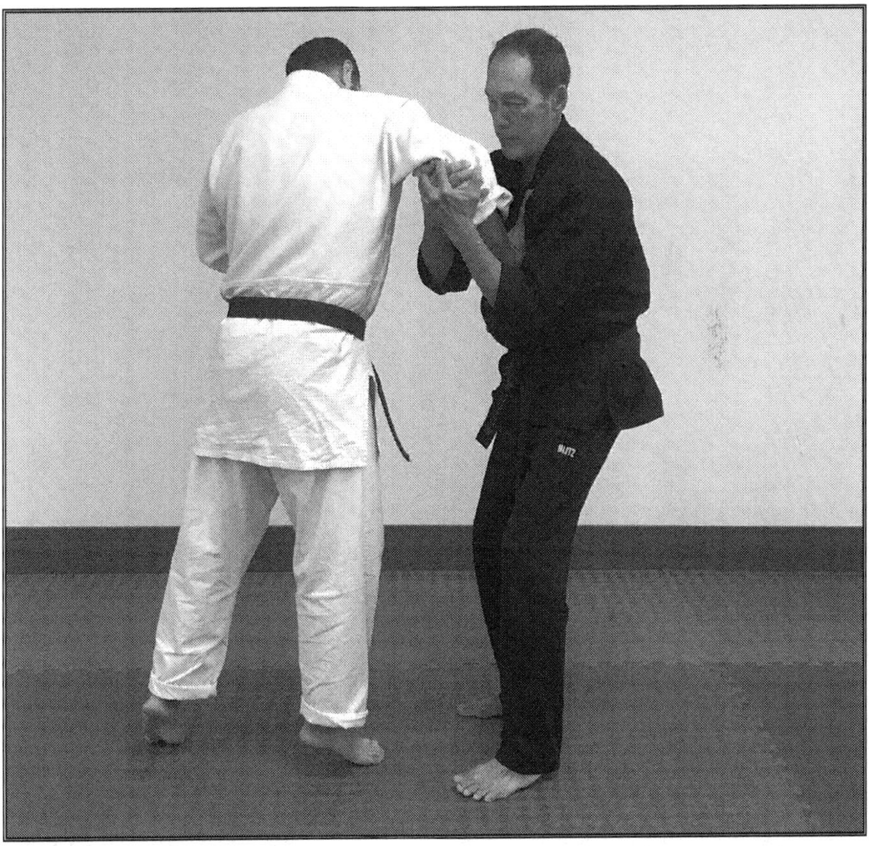

○ **Practice Pointer:** After the LH has trapped and 'positioned' uke's RH, it can assist tori's RH in cupping uke's elbow.

○ **Practice Pointer:** Because tori is committing both hands to trapping uke's RH, he must monitor pain compliance carefully to forestall a counter-strike with the free hand.

○ **Variation (One Handed):** This technique can be performed with the RH and LH working together, or the RH alone.

SMALL CIRCLE JUJITSU

As of the time of this writing [6/2020], the following is a list of the wrist locks from white to first degree black belt in the Small Circle Jujitsu system. As noted, however, this list is subject to change.

W-1 Basic Wrist Lock—*Kote Gaeshi*—Eighth Kyu

W-2 Reverse Wrist Lock—*Kote Mawashi*—Eighth Kyu

W-3 Bent Elbow Wrist Lock—*Kote Mawashi (Hiji)*—Seventh Kyu

W-4 Vertical Wrist Lock—*Kote Hineri*—Seventh Kyu

W-5 Underhand Wrist Lock—*(Gyaku) Kote Gaeshi*—Sixth Kyu

W-6 Handshake Wrist Lock—*Yubi Tori Shichi*—Sixth Kyu

W-7 Chicken Wing Lock—*Gyaku Tekubi Gatame*—Fifth Kyu

W-8 Goose Neck Lock—*Tekubi Gatame*—Fifth Kyu

W-9 Pistol Grip—*Oyayubi Gatame*—Fifth Kyu

Notes:_____

_____

_____

_____

_____

_____

_____

_____

_____

_____

SIGNS OF LIFE

Many years ago, Professor Wally was giving a seminar at a University in eastern Pennsylvania. One of the hosts at that event noticed that at the end of each practice set, a particular student would scurry over to the edge of the room and begin hurriedly jotting down notes in a book. Upon closer examination, this notebook was recognizable as Professor Wally's first book: Small Circle Jujitsu (O'Hara 1989), but it was only *just* recognizable as such: The cover was torn in several places; the spine was broken; the pages were stained with sweat and coffee and maybe even some blood; and throughout, cramped, multi-colored handwriting and crudely-drawn diagrams filled up every inch of empty space.

At first, the host was horrified to think that someone could treat such an important book in this cavalier fashion, and hoped that Professor Wally would not notice it. His own copy of this same book—autographed of course—occupied a place of pride on his bookshelf, and was in mint condition. But over time, the host came to realize that the pristine appearance of his book was due to lack of use, whereas the weathered appearance of the visitor's copy was the result of years of re-reading, annotating, studying, and interacting with the work.

It is the Editor's hope that in a few years, this book—in particular this appendix—will begin look more like the wise old visitor's copy than that of the naïve young host…

The foregoing techniques illustrate the principles—both old and new—that govern the art of Small Circle Jujitsu in action. Additional information regarding both the techniques and the principles may be found at:

www.smallcirclejujitsu.com

·◇· ACKNOWLEDGEMENTS ·◇·

As with any list of acknowledgments, there is a fair chance that the Editors will inadvertently neglect to mention kind and valuable contributions from one source or another. In an effort to avoid any such omission, it should be recognized that this work is, in its entirety, the product of the collaborative efforts of many of Professor Wally Jay's friends, family, students, and colleagues, and that each person whose name appears in this book has provided significant support to this special project. It is for this reason that authorship is collectively attributed to Wally Jay's family, friends and students. Having said that, it is appropriate to provide specific recognition for several individuals without whose assistance this work could not have been completed at all. Accordingly, special gratitude is extended to:

○ **Professor Leon Jay:** For allowing countless hours of unprecedented access to the very heart of the art.

○ **John Mellon:** Writing partner whose knowledge, wisdom, and connections in this realm remain unparalleled.

○ **Dr. Phil Courtney:** Medical/technical advisor, osteopath, and senior instructor for the Kenseikai in the UK who has been instrumental in the development of Small Circle Jujitsu for over three decades.

○ **Will Higginbotham:** Fountain of knowledge, true friend throughout the years, and perfect gentleman.

○ **Bill Troy:** Kind contributor who lives and proves his art on the mat.

○ **Dr. Charles Terry:** Wise mentor and guide along many pathways.

○ **John Ralston:** Patient and thoughtful editor and contributor.

○ **Dr. Harvey Levy:** Generous consultant who works at the intersection of harming and healing.